AA

MINI GUIDE

Peak District

D1324815

THE PENNINE WAY

Author: Mike Gerrard
Verifier: Neil Coates
Managing Editor: Paul Mitchell
Art Editor: Alison Fenton
Editor: Sandy Draper
Cartography provided by the Mapping Services Department of AA Publishing
Internal colour reproduction: Sarah Montgomery

Produced by AA Publishing
© Automobile Association Developments Limited 2007

Published by AA Publishing (a trading name of Automobile Association Developments Limited,
whose registered office is Fanum House, Basing View, Basingstoke, Hampshire RG21 4EA;
registered number 1878835).

 This product includes mapping data licensed from the Ordnance Survey®
with the permission of the Controller of Her Majesty's Stationery Office.
© Crown copyright 2007. All rights reserved. Licence number 100021153.

A03033F

TRADE ISBN-13: 978-0-7495-5587-0
SPECIAL ISBN-13: 978-0-7495-5694-5

A CIP catalogue record for this book is available from the British Library.

The contents of this book are believed correct at the time of printing. Nevertheless, the publishers
cannot be held responsible for any errors or omissions or for changes in the details given in this
book or for the consequences of any reliance on the information it provides. We have tried to ensure
accuracy in this book, but things do change and we would be grateful if readers would advise us of
any inaccuracies they may encounter. This does not affect your statutory rights.

Visit AA Publishing's website www.theAA.com/travel

Colour reproduction by Keene Group, Andover.
Printed in China by Everbest.

CONTENTS

It has been called the Hollow Country, an extraordinary landscape riven by gorges and riddled by caverns, where lowland England erupts into upland splendour, haltered by endless miles and countless acres of bronze-and-purple burnished moors, cliffs and scarps arcing to the horizon to meet with the lofty Pennines. The Peak District sits at the base of the Pennines, with one foot in the North and one in the Midlands. At its northern tip, the high moorlands merge seamlessly into the South Pennine massif dividing Yorkshire and Lancashire. In the south the graceful River Dove sparkles out of the limestone landscape, dividing Derbyshire and Staffordshire. Between these two contrasting images lies the Peak District National Park, a backyard playground for the city dwellers of the Midlands, Yorkshire and Manchester.

DOVEDALE

PUBLIC
FOOTPATH ONLY
MILLDALE
& DOVEDALE

Central England's first National Park, established in 1951, is the White Peak, reflecting the pale-grey hues of the limestone bedrock. Beyond the gaping maw of Dovedale are undulating plateaux dotted by prehistoric monuments and threaded by field walls; here ash woods cascade into spectacular valleys where seasonal rivers flow with crystal-clear water in winter and green veins of butterbur during summer. Beneath villages of silvery cottages set in abundant wild-flower meadows, miners toiled, turning the landscape inside-out, discovering cave systems and unwittingly creating heritage locations that merge into the background.

Around the north, east and west sweep escarpments and ridges of millstone grit, a rugged geological formation giving us the name of the Dark Peak. Vast moors dappled by reservoirs end in precipitous edges, over which waterfalls tumble into wooded vales that once echoed to the thrumming of industry. Here were the world's first great textile mills, England's own silk industry and countless other enterprises that make the Peak a peerless area for industrial archaeology. Tucked below the scalloped edges of these moors are small towns and villages of three-storey weaver's cottages and soot-darkened church towers, where a narrowboat offers a way to explore.

Traversing this former tribal domain – Peak comes from the Dark Ages clan, the *pecsaetan* – are Britain's first and latest National Trails, the Pennine Way and Pennine Bridleway. Myriad other trails combine with trekking country, cycling routes, many on former packhorse trails and railways.

Scratch the surface and the land that charmed and terrified authors and commentators from Daniel Defoe to George Eliot, Sir Arthur Conan Doyle to D H Lawrence is still there for the finding. The Hollow Country and its darker twin can enlighten and excite, educate and exhilarate. Enjoy every minute of it.

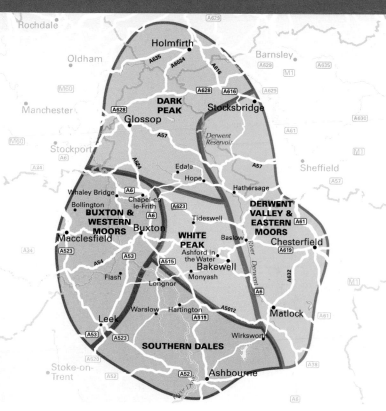

11

LADYBOWER RESERVOIR

ESSENTIAL SPOTS

Cycle along the twisting gorge of the Manifold Valley...go rock climbing at Ramshaw Rocks and Hen Cloud...wander around the elegant spa town of Buxton...visit the awesome Poole's Cavern...taste the famous pudding at Bakewell...explore romantic Haddon Hall or magnificent Chatsworth House ...follow in the footsteps of the Mass Trespass at Kinder Scout and discover wide open spaces where walkers, although close to large towns and cities, can feel as though they are at one with the wilderness.

2

1 Kinder Scout
A hiker tackles one of the large rock formations on the magnificent dark gritstone plateau of Kinder Scout, in the Dark Peak. Edale, at the start of the Pennine Way, is the access point to Kinder Scout.

2 The Roaches
Enjoy far-reaching views, which take in green fields divided by drystone walls while gentle slopes lead down to the valley bottom in the countryside near the Roaches.

3

4 Peak Cavern, Castleton
Peak Cavern is set into Castle Hill and has a natural entrance, 100 feet (30.5m) wide and 50 feet (15.2m) high. There are many exciting caves and mines to explore in the Peak District.

5 Ashbourne
Lively markets are a feature of many of the towns in the Peak District. In Ashbourne traders set up their stalls in Market Place on Thursdays.

3 Dovedale
This is one of the most beautiful, and popular of all the limestone dales, with paths, which range over windswept grassland hills to the deep shadows of the valley.

Day One in Peak District

For many people a weekend break or a long weekend is a popular way of spending their leisure time. These pages offer a loosely planned itinerary designed to ensure that you make the most of your time and see and enjoy the very best that the Peak District has to offer.

Friday Night

If you can afford it, stay at Fischer's Hotel, just north of Baslow village on the A623, perched above the River Derwent. The food is superb: herbs freshly picked from the kitchen garden and venison and lamb from the nearby Chatsworth Estate. In the evening you can go for a short drive and stroll on to Curbar Edge, for an exhilarating view of the setting sun over the White Peak.

Saturday Morning

On the A619 is the impressive entrance to Chatsworth Park. Spend the morning walking around the magnificent house and grounds, or explore East Moor and Beeley Moor. Here, you will fine excellent heather moorland, with Bronze Age settlements and barrows.

Return to Baslow and rejoin the A623, driving northwest up Middleton Dale, past Lovers' Leap and Baslow's tiny octagonal toll house.

LADYBOWER RESERVOIR

TIDESWELL

Saturday Lunch

Stop at the Three Stags Head pub at Wardlow Mires. This stone-floored pub serves well-kept beers from excellent independent Sheffield breweries. You'll find good food too, served on plates and dishes from the adjacent pottery.

Saturday Afternoon

Head for Tideswell, either by driving further along the A623 and turning off left, or by a side-road through the pretty village of Litton. Walk round the fine parish church at Tideswell ('Cathedral of the Peak') then take the car down to the Tideswell Dale car park and walk along Miller's Dale as far as Water-cum-Jolly Dale, with ash trees, limestone crags and the tinkling waters of the Wye.

Drive southwest on the B6049 and A5270 to meet the A515 and then go southeast to Parsley Hay. Turn left on minor roads for Youlgreave for a look at the great stone circle of Arbor Low – a ditch, bank and circle of 47 stones, now lying flat – and the nearby barrow of Gib Hill; both date from the Bronze Age. Return to the A515 and turn left; then right onto the B5054 to Hartington.

Saturday Night

Stay at Biggin Hall, located just a mile (1.6km) to the southeast of Hartington; it comprises a cluster of 17th-century buildings with mullioned windows and oak beams. If possible, try to book the Master Suite, complete with four-poster bed. In the morning, enjoy a traditional farmhouse breakfast using good locally produced ingredients.

Day Two in Peak District

Today, you are in the heart of the White Peak, close to the southern dales. Your second day explores this beautiful area before heading north for a tour of the Dark Peak, with alternative options depending on your personal preferences and, of course, the weather.

Sunday Morning

Go for an early walk down Biggin Dale, or linger over breakfast and then look round Hartington; feed the ducks on the pond and buy some local Stilton to take home. Then follow in the footsteps of the *'Compleat Anglers'*, Izaak Walton and Charles Cotton, down Beresford Dale on the quiet upper reaches of the River Dove. You can walk as far as you wish, into Wolfscote Dale and to Mill Dale, but for this you will need a packed lunch.

Further south still is famous Dovedale. If you wish you can drive to Ilam and take the easy short walk by the Stepping Stones to Mill Dale. But remember, this route is likely to be popular on a fine Sunday morning.

Sunday Lunch

From Hartington or Ilam head for Warslow (on the B5053), where you can call in for lunch at the Greyhound Inn, a traditional coaching inn popular for its home-cooked dishes. Warslow is close to the Manifold Valley; a short detour down minor roads into Ecton will give you a flavour of the scenery.

WINNATS PASS, CASTLETON

Sunday Afternoon

Leaving Warslow, drive north on the A5053 to and through Longnor to reach the A515; here turn left to reach the market town of Buxton.

There are now several options. If the weather is really unkind you can spend the afternoon here, breezing around the Pavilion Gardens or visiting Poole's Cavern. Return to Baslow via the A6 south, Bakewell and then the A619.

Alternatively, head north on the A6 through Dove Holes, turn right onto the A623 and then fork left at The Wanted Inn to reach Castleton via the dramatic Winnats Pass road. In Castleton, there are caves and Blue John mines, the oldest castle in the Peak and good pubs and cafés.

Or, if you are feeling adventurous and there is no risk of blizzards stay on the A6 north to Chapel-en-le-Frith then north on the A624 to Glossop. Turn east on the A57, crossing the Snake Pass and dropping down the Woodlands Valley to the Derwent Dams. Whichever way you go, finish at Padley Gorge (Grindleford) close to where you started, in the shade of sessile oaks and with pied flycatchers singing among the branches.

TISSINGTON

Southern Dales

ASHBOURNE

CARSINGTON WATER

DOVEDALE

HARTINGTON

ILAM

LONGNOR

MANIFOLD VALLEY

TISSINGTON

WIRKSWORTH

INTRODUCTION

The arc of countryside from Leek through Ashbourne to Belper rolls and dips southwards to the river plain and its tributary, the Dove, meanders through fields and hedgerows. But on the far side of Ashbourne everything changes as the land rises and the Dove spreads out a thousand fingers into every crevice of the hills. Brooks and rivulets reach into the limestone at the Peak's core. Villages lie on the thousand-foot contour on the plateau because the valleys are so narrow; ancient ash woods clothe the slopes, cattle graze the pastures and drystone walls cobweb the meadows.

DOVEDALE

HOT SPOTS

Unmissable attractions

Explore the old market town of Ashbourne, celebrated for its delicious gingerbread, at the gateway to Dovedale...explore the quieter, reef limestone hills of Chrome and High Wheeldone from the little hilltop village of Longnor...cycle along the twisting gorge of the Manifold Valley, which has one of several cycle rides that follow the tracks of disused railways...go windsurfing or birdwatching at Carsington Water...taste Buxton Blue, White Stilton and Dovedale at the Hartington Creamery...explore the lovely parkland that surrounds the Ilam Estate...admire the dressed wells at Tissington throughout the late spring and summer.

1

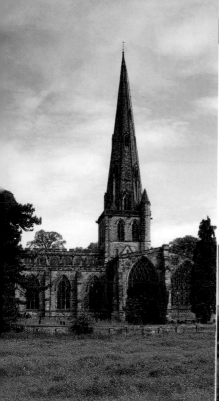

1 Dovedale
A path follows the River Dove as it winds its way below the dramatic limestone peaks.

2 Ashbourne
St Oswald's Church in Ashbourne with its tall spire (212 feet/65m), is one of Derbyshire's grandest.

3 Manifold Valley
Thor's Cave dominates the centre of the Manifold Valley.

ASHBOURNE

The old market town of Ashbourne is located in a cleft in the rolling farmland of southwest Derbyshire, a landscape of fields and hedges rather than moors and walls. Along this cleft runs the Henmore Brook on its way to meet the River Dove.

The drive into and through Ashbourne is not straightforward; there is a one-way system and the roads are often congested, but there are points on the sweeping drive down into the town where the shape of the settlement can be appreciated. The most immediate impression is that the parish church, with its distinctive needle-sharp spire, is some way from the town centre. This means there is a walk of several hundred yards if you want to take a closer look at St Oswald's, but by doing so, and exploring the Market Place on the way, you see the very best of the town.

Ashbourne Market Place, opposite the Town Hall, used to be lined with alehouses and, at one

Visit

'OAKBOURNE'

Ashbourne is a perfect example of an English market town – eccentric street plan, narrow cobbled alleys, coaching inns, almshouses and market stalls. It needed very little alteration to become George Eliot's Oakbourne in *Adam Bede*, and is probably the best place in the Peak District to explore for antiques (but don't expect many bargains!).

time, had its own bullring (close to the Wright Memorial, an elaborate piece of Victoriana). It was here that Bonnie Prince Charlie proclaimed his father King of England, and it was from here that the famous Shrovetide Football, between the 'Uppards' and 'Downards' of the town, always started. It was moved to Shaw Croft to reduce damage to property, but still rages along the Henmore, between the goals of Sturton Mill and Clifton Mill, each Easter. At the back of the Market

Place is the Old Vaults pub, which used to be called The Anatomical Horse, with a skeleton for its sign. Down the narrow alley to the left is Victoria Square (once The Butchery and The Shambles) and Tiger Yard, beside a restaurant that used to be The Tiger Inn. The modern Victoria Square is a smart little suntrap, set about with benches.

Ashbourne's side streets and alleys are narrow and interesting; the layout of the old town north of the Henmore dates back to the 11th and 12th centuries and there are some fascinating nooks and crannies to explore, such as Lovatt's Yard and the House of Confinement (a lock-up) on Bellevue Street. However, it is along St John's Street and Church Street that the town's grandest buildings are to be found. Beyond the Clergy's Widows Almshouses are superb mansions and merchants' houses, several now serving as antiques shops, culminating in the magnificent stone-gabled Grammar School,

founded by Elizabeth I in 1585. And opposite, set behind tall wrought-iron gates and a carpet of daffodils in the spring, stands St Oswald's. It was built around 1340 and perfectly described by the novelist George Eliot as 'the finest mere parish church in England'.

CARSINGTON WATER

New reservoirs usually take years to blend with a landscape, and sometimes they never do. Carsington, opened by Her Majesty the Queen in 1992, already looks at home in the gently rolling hills southwest of Wirksworth.

Most of the Peak District's many reservoirs gather their water from acid moorland, so they are low in nutrients, and this in turn means they are poor for aquatic plants and animals. However, Carsington is quite different: it is filled largely by water pumped from rivers and so is excellent for wildlife. In the winter there are wildfowl by the thousand, including widgeon, pochard and

Insight

THE RUDDY DUCK

One of Carsington Water's controversial residents is the American ruddy duck. Just fifty years ago this little duck (it has a big blue bill, white cheeks, a reddish back and a stiff tail) was quite unknown outside the Wildfowl Trust, but it escaped and is now so widespread that it is threatening to overrun Europe, diluting the genes of its close relative the European white-headed duck in the process.

tufted duck; in the summer there are great crested grebes and dabchicks; and at migration time, all sorts of waders and seabirds use the reservoir as an oasis on their way from coast to coast.

A third of the Carsington shore is set aside as a conservation area, but the rest is accessible by footpath, by bicycle and by horse. The main Visitor Centre is on the west shore, with an extensive car park (pay and display) off the B5035.

There are several mining villages to the north of Carsington Water, including Brassington, which boasts 18th-century houses and a Norman church. Inside the church, look for the even older carving high on the west wall of the tower of a naked man with his hands on his heart.

Hopton village is now dominated by the reservoir, though there is a bypass. Until 1989 Hopton Hall (not open) was the home of the Gell family, who made their fortune from the nearby limestone quarries, and their name as scholars, politicians and travellers. Along the limestone rise to the north runs the Hopton Incline, once the steepest gradient for any standard-gauge railway line in Britain, using fixed engines and cable-haulage to set the High Peak Railway on its journey from Cromford Wharf to Whaley Bridge. It is now the High Peak Trail. Further north again is the Via Gellia, a road created and named by one of the Gells, through flower-rich woodland along a valley west of Cromford.

DOVEDALE

Fame, beauty and availability are a heady mix. Dovedale's Stepping Stones appear on a thousand postcards and attract a million visitors, all of whom seem to be queuing to cross the crystal waters of the Dove at the same time. The National Trust does a heroic job to manage this part of its South Peak Estate, but it's still a good idea to keep away on sunny Sundays.

The Dove flows for 45 miles (72.4km), but only a short section of it is called Dovedale; above the Viator Bridge it becomes Mill Dale, then Wolfscote Dale and then Beresford Dale. But it is to the gorge of Dovedale that the visitors flock, for within the space of a few miles of easy riverside walking, on a broad level path, there are superb craggy rocks and pillars (all named) rising out of dense ash woodland, sweeps of open pasture, banks of flowers, dark caves and cascades of spring water. There is no road, and only one main path, following the east bank.

Insight

NATURE RETURNED

Just north of Carsington and Hopton the landscape rises to a 1,000-foot (305m) contour, topped by a stone called King's Chair. This area is pockmarked by old lead mines and limestone quarries, but wild flowers abound on the open limestone and into the Via Gellia; in places several kinds of orchid jostle for space, and in ash woodland there are patches of the rare herb Paris quadrifolia.

It is not even necessary to cross the stepping stones upstream from the car park on the Staffordshire side of the river, because there is a footbridge a few yards away.

Victorian fashion blighted Dovedale; it was praised by every famous romantic writer from Byron to Tennyson and was soon as popular as Switzerland. Donkey tours and guided expeditions once ferried people up the path to view the scenery. Of more enduring merit

Insight

PLOUGHMAN'S PARADISE

The cheese shop at Hartington sells produce from the nearby Hartington Creamery, which was established in the 1870s and began making Stilton in the 1920s. Specialities include Buxton Blue, White Stilton and Dovedale, a relatively new cheese, which is as delicious as any of the more traditional varieties. The local pubs often sell beers brewed at the tiny Whim Brewery, based on a remote farm near the village. Truly a ploughman's dream come true!

were the earlier words of Izaak Walton, who loved the Dove and put his head and heart into writing *The Compleat Angler*.

HARTINGTON

Hartington is a tourist honeypot but, like Tissington and Ashford, there is enough in the fabric and culture of the village to cope with popularity and still have a heart. Curiously, its heart is probably the duck pond, or mere, which sits like a round pearl in a circlet of duck-cropped lawn. Nearby is Ye Olde Cheese Shoppe, selling superb local Stilton. Just a stone's-throw away are tea rooms, shops, a pottery and two pubs – old coaching inns from the days when Hartington was a significant market town. One has the unusual name, The Charles Cotton, after the angling resident of Beresford Hall, friend and collaborator of Izaak Walton. It was on the upper reaches of the Dove as it flowed below Beresford Hall that Cotton and Walton perfected their arts and gathered their fishing stories, published in 1653 as *The Compleat Angler*.

Just out of the village, up a steep side road to the east, is Hartington Hall, a sturdy yeoman's manor built in the 17th century. It was the home of the Bateman family but has been a youth hostel since 1934. Also to the east of the village is a signal box of the Ashbourne–Buxton Railway, which closed in 1967 and is now an

information centre on the Tissington Trail, whilst 3 miles (4.8km) north is Pilsbury Castle, a mound probably on the site of an Iron Age fort.

Hartington occupies a strategic position for walkers and explorers of the less obvious paths and byways. To the east and the west lie dry valleys and a lattice of green pastures and to the south is Beresford Dale.

ILAM

On most maps the River Manifold can be traced in a blue line, flowing south from Longnor to meet the Dove 1 mile (1.6km) below Ilam. In fact this is not usually what happens, and, like several other celebrated rivers in limestone country, the Manifold has a secret life, flowing underground unless the water table is high. Below Wettonmill the river abruptly disappears and takes almost 24 hours to resurface, at the Boil Holes in the grounds of Ilam Hall. This explains why there are no footpaths along what appears on paper to be a pretty section of the lower valley. This does not mean the landscape isn't interesting, but there is no focal point, and the footpaths linking to the old halls of Throwley and Castern on the upper slopes of the valley are rarely walked.

Ilam, above the confluence of two famous rivers, has always been an important settlement, but never very large. Originally it belonged to Burton Abbey, but after the Reformation the estate was divided among three families, the Ports of Ilam Hall, the Meverells of Throwley and the Hurts of Castern. Of these the Meverells no longer exist and Throwley Hall is a ruin; the Ports sold Ilam to Jesse Watts Russell in the early 19th century, and the Hurts still live at secluded Castern.

Alas, Russell swept away most of old Ilam and built a model village, the buildings of which have the look of a Swiss cuckoo clock. Ilam Hall was rebuilt on a grand scale; a quarter of it remains and is used as a youth hostel. The lovely parkland that surrounds it is open to the public. Close by is the church, totally rebuilt, but with two fragments from Saxon crosses and a Tudor chapel with a shrine to the local medieval hermit St Bertram.

The Ilam estate passed to the National Trust in 1934 and is a popular destination for day visitors, because of its pleasant walks and its close proximity to Dovedale.It has literary associations with Boswell, Johnson and Izaak Walton.

LONGNOR

The fate of Longnor was sealed by the demise of the turnpikes and lack of a railway link; its worthy ambition to be a proper market town withered away. It stands now in the no man's land that lies between the Manifold and the Dove, but at a pivotal point in the Peak District. Around it lie strip fields dating back to medieval times; just to the north lies Derbyshire and the limestone knoll country, whilst to the west are the darker gritstone hills of Staffordshire.

The Manifold at Longnor is no more than a babbling brook, but the valley is broad, with meadows and sandstone barns. Yellowhammers and whitethroats sing from the thorn bushes; swallows swoop for insects over the reed-grass. Longnor presides over the long, straight road like a drowsy cat over a barn floor. The village is pretty and compact, with a little square and a Victorian market hall. A stone inscription above the entrance carries the tariff of ancient market tolls.

MANIFOLD VALLEY

The Manifold and the Dove rise within a mile (1.6km) of each other below Axe Edge. As they head southeast together into limestone country, twisting and side-winding like pulled strands of wool, one is transmuted into a Staffordshire valley, the other into a Derbyshire dale. The difference in landscape terms is quite minimal; they both cut a course through superb scenery, meeting finally at Ilam, yet the

Manifold Valley escaped all the Victorian hype and the more carnival atmosphere of Dovedale.

Wetton and Warslow villages, on the 1000-foot (305m) contour on opposite sides of the valley, are the main access points for the most dramatic section of the Manifold. Neither makes very much concession to tourists, though both have good pubs (the Olde Royal Oak and the Greyhound). Warslow has a utilitarian look, as do its medieval iron stocks close to the school. It is an estate village of the Crewe family (of Calke Abbey, south of Derby) and lies at the very foot of the gritstone moors, which can be reached by taking the side road to the northwest. Wetton is on the limestone, among dairy farms and barns, but its stout church and many of its cottages look as if they belong amongst heather.

A steep side road north of Warslow off the B5053 drops down to Ecton, and the most beautiful section of the valley begins. It runs southwards along a thin strip of level meadow, with steep, flower-studded, almost alpine-looking, grassland on either side. The road, and what is now the Manifold Trail, follows the route of the Leek and Manifold Valley Light Railway, which opened in 1904 but only survived for 30 years; according to expert judgement it opened too late and closed too soon – if its odd Indian-style engines were still running today the line would make a fortune!

Close by to Wettonmill the Manifold usually disappears down swallow-holes, travelling all the rest of the way to Ilam underground. Meanwhile, the Manifold's tributary, the Hamps, heads southwards and the Manifold Trail stays with the old railway line, going along the Hamps to the large village of Waterhouses.

Once out of the depth of the valley, the steep limestone hill slopes are pockmarked with deep caves. The most famous is Thor's Cave but several others, such as Ossom's Cave and Elderbush, have

45

THOR'S CAVE, MANIFOLD VALLEY

Insight & Visit

WELL DRESSING

The most famous and picturesque of all the Peak District traditions, well dressing, probably has its roots in pagan ceremonies to placate water spirits, but the Christian version has its origins at Tissington, where the five wells ran with pure water through the years of the Black Death. The villagers believed they owed their lives to the water, and dressed the tops of the wells as a sign of thanksgiving. Well dressings take place throughout the late spring and summer.

Activity

THE TISSINGTON TRAIL

The famous Tissington Trail runs for 13 miles (20.9km) from Parsley Hay to Ashbourne, along the old railway line which closed in 1963. You will find that the trail is particularly suitable for families and cyclists who appreciate a car-free countryside; it is possible to hire bikes at either Parsley Hay or Ashbourne, or bring your own and leave your car at the car park, on the site of the old railway station.

been explored or excavated and have produced bones and flints from the Stone and Bronze Ages, when this was good hunting country. All the domed hills, which are called Lows, are capped by cairns or barrows and it is very easy on the dry 'karst' hillsides to imagine yourself in another older world.

TISSINGTON

Tissington is a gem, too beautiful for its own good on summer Sundays. The classic approach is off the A515, through a gateway and over a cattle grid, then along a drive lined with lime trees. The original avenue, of venerable pollards and tall standards, has recently been felled, but there are rows of young trees set further back. Into the village itself, past a walled yew and the first of several wells, sandstone cottages are set back behind wide grass verges and shaded by elegant beeches. There is a village green, with the stream running through it, a duck pond complete with ducks,

TISSINGTON

TISSINGTON HALL

a Norman church and a grand Jacobean Hall. This is, and has been for centuries, an idyllic, well-managed estate village.

Tissington Hall, low and wide with mullioned windows and tall chimneys, is the home of the Fitzherbert family. It is set behind a low wall and gate of fine wrought ironwork (by Robert Bakewell).

The overwhelming impression of Tissington is of its perfect blend of old stone houses, trees and water. Every wall is draped in flowers and creepers. A few decades ago there would have been the sound of steam trains, but the line closed in 1963 and the trackway is now a walk/cycle/horse-riding route, managed by the National Park Authority and known as the Tissington Trail.

A few miles southwest along the Tissington Trail, beside the A515, is the village of Fenny Bentley. The village is dominated by a square 15th-century tower, incorporated into the more recent Cherry Orchard Farm. The tower was part of the old Hall, the home of the Beresford family, and in St Edmund's Church is an alabaster tomb to Thomas Beresford and his family. Thomas fought at Agincourt with eight of his sons; these, together with his wife and their further 14 children, are depicted on and around the tomb as bodies wrapped in shrouds, probably because by the time the tomb was built nobody would have known what they had looked like.

WIRKSWORTH

A few years ago Wirksworth was a town of quarry dust and fusty alleys. Now it is a fascinating places to visit, full of history, neat and welcoming. This shows what can happen with a little vision and civic enthusiasm, but there is a suspicion that the hard edges of Wirksworth's past, as a lead-mining and quarrying centre, have been smoothed away rather than dusted off. The lead mining industry disappeared many years ago, to be replaced by quarrying, which is still of considerable local importance. The National Stone Centre just outside the town gives a fuller picture. Nearby is the old quarry of Black Rock, a picnic spot with a 4-mile (6.4km) forest trail over Cromford Moor and access to the High Peak Trail (the old railway line that transported stone to the Cromford Canal).

The Market Place and car park, is a good place to start exploring the town. Up Dale End there are wickedly sloping lanes with cobbled gutters, leading past the old smithy, opposite Green Hill, a 17th-century gabled house built of limestone with sandstone mullioned windows. Further up the hill is Babington House (not open), of similar vintage, set in a pretty garden and with a view over the town. It is a three-storey residence, with a stone sundial on the gable wall.

South from the Market Place, past the Town Hall, is Coldwell Street with several old inns, including The Red Lion, The Vaults, which were originally called The Compleat Angler, and The George. Down Chapel Lane is Moot Hall (not open), the only place in England where lead-miners' Barmote Courts (to settle any lead-mining disputes) are still held (they started here in 1266, though this building only dates back to 1814). Inside there is a Miners Standard Dish, dated 1513, which was used for measuring the ore, as a levy had to be paid to both the King and the Barmaster who was in charge of the court. The Barmote Court still sits twice a year.

Hidden away behind the fronts of tall houses is St Mary's Church. It is accessible along Church Street or through the old alley of the lychgate, of which only the tall stone pillars remain. The grassed churchyard is encircled by iron railings, which separate it from a narrow lane called Church Walk, and a jumble of back yards and sloping roofs. The church itself is broad and solid with an eccentrically tiny spire or spike, as if all but the top few feet had fallen through the roof of the tower.

SOUTHERN DALES

TOURIST INFORMATION CENTRE
Ashbourne
13 The Market Place.
Tel: 01335 343666

PLACES OF INTEREST
Derwent Crystal
Shawcroft, Ashbourne.
Tel: 01335 345219
Ecclesbourne Valley Railway
Wirksworth Station.
Tel: 01629 823076;
www.evra.org.uk
High Peak Junction Workshops
Wirksworth.
Tel: 01629 822831
Original workshops, railway exhibition
and information centre.
Ilam Park
4.5 miles (7.2km) northwest of
Ashbourne. Woods and parkland on
the banks of the River Manifold.
Middleton Top Engine House
Middleton Top Visitor Centre,
Middleton by Wirksworth.
Tel: 01629 823204
Engine house with a beam engine to
haul wagons up the Middleton incline.

National Stone Centre
Porter Lane, Wirksworth.
Tel: 01629 824833;
www.nationalstonecentre.org
Exhibition, guided walks and gem
panning.
Steeple Grange Light Railway
The Quarry Men's Line,
Middleton by Wirksworth.
Tel: 01246 205542;
www.steeplegrange.co.uk
Rides every ten minutes.
Wirksworth Heritage Centre
Crown Yard.
Tel: 01629 825225;
www.gilkin.demon.co.uk
Former silk and velvet mill with
displays illustrating the town's history.

SHOPPING
Ashbourne
Antiques shops in Church Street.
General market, Thu.
Cattle market, Sat.
Wirksworth
General market, Tue.

LOCAL SPECIALITIES

Cheeses
Local cheeses, including blue
Stilton, from Ye Olde Cheese Shoppe,
Hartington.
Tel: 01298 84935;
www.hartingtoncheese.co.uk
Dove Dairy, Hartington.
Tel: 01298 84496

Crafts
Longnor Craft Centre, The Market Hall,
Longnor.
Tel: 01298 83587

Honey
Daisybank Apiaries, Newtown, Longnor.
Tel: 01298 83526
Peak District honey, mead.

Pottery
Rooke's, 1 Mill Lane, Hartington
Tel: 01298 84650;
www.rookespottery.co.uk

SPORTS & ACTIVITIES

ANGLING
Fly Fishing
Carsington Water.
Tel: 01629 540696;
www.stwater.co.uk

BOAT HIRE
Carsington Water.
Tel: 01629 540478;
www.carsingtonwater.com

CYCLING *SEE* LONG-DISTANCE FOOTPATHS & TRAILS

CYCLE HIRE
(For those marked P, website is
www.peakdistrict.org)

Ashbourne (P)
Ashbourne Cycle Hire Centre,
Mapleton Lane.
Tel: 01335 343156

Carsington Water
Tel: 01629 540696;
www.stwater.co.uk

Middleton Top (P)
Visitor Centre, Middleton by
Wirksworth.
Tel: 01629 823204

Parsley Hay (P)
Peak District National Park Centre,
Waterhouses.
Tel: 01298 84493

Brown End Farm Cycle Hire
BrownEndFarm.
Tel: 01538 308313;
www.users.zetnet.co.uk

55

Manifold Valley Bike Hire
Earls Way, Old Station Car Park.
Tel: 01538 308609;
www.manifoldvalleybikes.com

GUIDED WALKS

Derbyshire Dales Countryside Service
Planning and Development Services,
Town Hall, Matlock.
Full guided walks service.
Tel: 01629 761326

National Park Walks with a Ranger
Peak District National Park.
Tel: 01629 816200;
www.peakdistrict.org.uk

Peak District
Annual Peak District Walking Festival.
Guided walks April/May.
Tel: 0870 444 7275;
www.visitpeakdistrict.com/walk

Wirksworth & Peak District
Professional Blue Badge Guides.
Tel: 01629 584284

HANG-GLIDING

Alstonefield
Adrenaline High Adventure Sports,
the Old Vicarage, Wetton, near
Ashbourne.
Tel: 01335 310296

Ashbourne
The Peak School of Hang Gliding,
The Elms, Wetton.
Tel: 01335 310257

HORSE-RIDING

Tissington Trekking Centre
Tissington Wood Farm, Ashbourne.
Tel: 01335 350276

LONG-DISTANCE
FOOTPATHS & TRAILS

The High Peak Trail
Follows the former High Peak Railway
from High Peak Junction (Cromford) to
Dowlow (south of Buxton). Derbyshire
Countryside Centre.
Tel: 01629 823204

Manifold Trail
Traces a former narrow-gauge railway
from Hulme End to Waterhouses,
8.25 miles (13km) of walking or cycling.
Visitor Centre at Hulme End.

The Tissington Trail
Part of old Ashbourne– Buxton railway.
Runs for 13 miles (21km) alongside
Dovedale from Ashbourne, and joins
the High Peak Trail near Parsley Hay.
Derbyshire Countryside Centre.
Tel: 01629 823204

WATERSPORTS

Carsington Water, near Ashbourne.
Tel: 01629 540478;
www.carsingtonwater.com

ANNUAL EVENTS & CUSTOMS

For the full programme visit
www.visitpeakdistrict.com

Ashbourne

Shrovetide Football, Shrove
Tue–Ash Wed.
Highland Gathering, with parade of
pipe bands, mid-Jul.
Ashbourne Show, late Aug.
Well dressing (Wynaston & Mayfield),
mid-Jun.

Bonsall

Hen racing, The Barley Mow pub,
mid-Aug.

Dovedale

The Dovedale Dash, a 4.25-mile
(6.8km) cross-country run which starts
on Thorpe Pastures, early Nov.

Hartington

Well dressing, Sep.

Ilam

Manifold Valley Agricultural Show,
The Arbour, Castern Hall Farm,
early Aug.
Dovedale Sheepdog Trials, mid-Aug.

Longnor

Well dressing and Wakes, early Sep.
Longnor Races, Sep.

Tissington

Well dressing, Ascension Day.
Wetton.
Official World Toe Wrestling
Championships, (Olde Red Lion Inn),
early Jun.

Wirksworth

Well dressing, late May.
Clypping of the Church service, early
Sep.
Festival of Music and Arts, Sep.

TEA ROOMS

Bassett Wood Farm
Tissington, Ashbourne,
Derbyshire, DE6 1RD
Tel: 01335 350254
www.bassettwoodfarm.co.uk
This friendly, welcoming and informal
tea room set in a working farmhouse
is always heady with the rich aroma of
home-baking. Look out for local jams,
honey and dairy produce and indulge in
tasty ice creams.

Beresford Tea Room
Market Place, Hartington,
Derbyshire, SK17 0AL
Tel: 01298 84418
This tea room is also the village post
office. As ever, local produce and local
baking is to the fore; try some of the
local Hartington Stilton (maybe on a
chilli oatcake). In the winter months,
the hotpot is particularly welcoming.

Manifold Tearooms
Ilam Hall, Ilam,
Staffordshire, DE6 2AZ
Tel: 01335 350245
The stable block to the Hall (a Youth
Hostel) is now a National Trust tea
room with an emphasis on vegetarian
and organic foods. Enjoy tea and cakes
or try one of the more substantial
meals. The local cheeses are also
excellent and worth sampling.

Craft Centre Coffee Shop
Longnor Market Hall, Longnor,
Staffordshire, SK17 0N
Tel: 01298 83587
This enterprising little café serves
a variety of delicious home-baked
produce including Staffordshire
oatcakes. The little Victorian Market
Hall is also home to locally made art
and crafts, all for sale.

DOVEDALE

TISSINGTON

The George Inn
Alstonefield, Ashbourne,
Staffordshire, DE6 2FX
Tel: 01335 310205

The George has beamed rooms, quarry-tile floors and log fires, old photos and polished plate. You'll find dilling, home-made pub food and a couple of real ales from regional breweries. On hot summer days, shelter in the cool courtyard beneath an immense ash tree.

Ye Olde Gate Inn
Well Street, Brassington,
Derbyshire, DE4 4HJ
Tel: 01629 540228

This is a tremendous old pub – haunted of course – with lovely low-dark beams (salvaged from an Armada ship), old blackened ranges, quarry-tile floors, old settles and pews and a superbly atmospheric snug. There's grand local fodder and several real ales to enjoy.

The Pack Horse Inn
Crowdecote, near Buxton,
Derbyshire, SK17 0DB
Tel: 01298 83618

Set in a tiny hamlet above the upper Dove Valley, with small rooms, simply furnished, sitting beneath a higgledy-piggledy roof. Enjoy the fine quality, ever-changing food menu of tasty dishes and beers from local microbreweries in the lovely raised beer-garden.

The Barley Mow
The Dale, Bonsall, Cromford,
Derbyshire, DE4 2AY
Tel: 01629 825685
www.barleymowbonsall.co.uk

The friendly landlord tells tales of UFOs, ghosts and ghouls at this old village pub, with its warm winter fires, grand, home-cooked food, locally brewed beers and an unspoilt interior.

MACCLESFIELD FOREST

Buxton &
Western Moors

INTRODUCTION

Macclesfield and Leek mark the western and southern edges of the Peak uplands: to the north are Whaley Bridge and Chapel-en-le-Frith. In between are truly dramatic gritstone outcrops and windswept heather moors. Two rivers drain the watershed: to the north the Goyt, rising on the peaty slopes of the Cat and Fiddle Moor; to the south the pretty River Dane. To the east of all this is the grand spa town of Buxton.

THE ROACHES

HOT SPOTS

Unmissable attractions

Visit Leek built on the profits of the silk industry and where the first hills of the Peak District rise up from the Staffordshire Plains...go hang gliding or rock climbing or wallaby-spotting at the Roaches, a dramatic millstone grit outcrop...go shopping and enjoy the waters at the elegant spa town of Buxton...explore the awesome gulf of Poole's Cavern, the Peak's most accessible cave for intrepid explorers...go fishing or sailing on Errwood Reservoir in the magnificent Goyt Valley...hire a canal boat and float down river at Whaley Bridge...admire the Palladian grandeur of Lyme Park, which featured as 'Pemberley' in the recent BBC adaptation of *Pride and Prejudice*...go walking in Tegg's Nose Country Park, Cheshire.

1 Errwood Reservoir, Goyt Valley

It looks as if it has always been here, but Errwood Reservoir is a relatively recent addition to the valley landscape, along with its neighbour Fernilee. Built by Stockport Corporation, Fernilee was flooded in 1938 and Errwood followed in 1967. The Forestry Commission added woodlands in the 1960s. A fly-fishing club and a sailing club both make use of Errwood Reservoir.

2 Buxton

Situated in the Pavilion Gardens, on the banks of the River Wye, the impressive domed Octagon was first opened to the public in 1876. This magnificent glass and cast-iron structure today operates as an auction house and also hosts antiques and collectors' fairs.

3 Whaley Bridge

The Peak Forest Canal ends at the picturesque Whaley Bridge canal basin. Colourful longboats and the tow path provide a leisurely way to explore.

Insight

THE BEST BREW

Local people still queue up at St Ann's Well to fill plastic containers with the tepid water, claiming it makes the best tea in Britain. Try it straight from the well. It was good enough for Mary, Queen of Scots, and it was water that brought the Romans into the Peak District in the first place.

BUXTON

Dropping down from the high moors into the elegant spa town of Buxton, on the River Wye, is enough to make anyone blink in disbelief as they find themselves emerging out of the bleak wilderness into a bower of parks and gardens and grand Palladian-style buildings.

Through the centuries health resorts have sprung up in all sorts of unlikely places, and none more so than Buxton. The Romans, who had a passion for bathing, established a rest or leisure facility here in the days of Agricola, when the frontier fighting had shifted north to Caledonia and this was a safe haven with the additional benefit of natural warm springs. After the Romans left, the Christians came to take the 'cripple's cure' at St Ann's Well and to pray for miracles.

By the 18th century Buxton, in common with other spa towns, was set firmly on the fashion trail. The 5th Duke of Devonshire was responsible for the main wave of building innovation at Buxton. He had been impressed in the 1770s by the Royal Crescent at Bath and was awash with money from his Ecton copper mines. First he had the elegant semicircular Crescent built, complete with 42 pilasters and 378 windows, then the Great Stable with a central court and Tuscan columns, finally followed by Hall Bank and The Square, all built in a grand and imposing style.

In the 19th century the 6th and 7th Dukes carried on the work, so that by late Victorian times the spa in the valley had completely

Insight

HEATHER ON THE MOORS

Common heather, or ling, turns the moors purple in August, but there are two other kinds of heather on the hills around Buxton – cross-leaved heather found on wet or boggy ground and bell-heather found on dry, rocky slopes. Both these plants have bigger flowers than the common heather, but don't attract as many bees. Heather honey is a local speciality and tastes wonderful, spread on freshly baked bread.

eclipsed the old market town on the upper slope. The Great Stable became the Devonshire Hospital, 'for the use of the sick poor', and was given a massive domed roof 156 feet (47.4m) across (it is now part of The University of Derby); terraces of hotels and guest houses sprang up to cater for the influx of affluent visitors to the Thermal and Natural Baths; the railways arrived, the beautiful Pavilion Gardens were laid out on the banks of the Wye, and in 1905 the magnificent Opera House was opened to audiences.

Surprisingly, the majority of Buxton's fine buildings are still functioning and thriving. The Edwardian Opera House has a full programme, taking advantage of the current interest in opera. Outside is an immaculate square, complete with an ornate Victorian post box, and behind it run the Pavilion Gardens with a Serpentine Walk.

Perhaps the best way to soak up the town's authentic atmosphere is to park your car at the market place in the old town (it vies with Alston in Cumbria in its claim to be the highest market town in England) and walk past the town hall, down a path across the grassy dome called The Slopes towards the Crescent. Few places in England evoke such a comfortable, Pre-Raphaelite sense of town and country. Plenty of shopping arcades keep the streets lively and local businesses thriving. There are weekly markets and you

OPERA HOUSE

DRESS CIRCLE AND STALLS

PAVILION GARDENS, BUXTON

will find the Tourist Information Centre on the site of the original mineral baths. Opposite The Crescent is the famous twin-domed old Pump Room, where smart visitors once took their prescribed mineral waters. Nearby stands a modest fountain, which is the source of the famous waters and of Buxton's continued prosperity.

CHAPEL-EN-LE-FRITH

Unfortunately, a pretty name does not always describe a picturesque place. The frith, or forest, never really existed except to formalise a vast tract of Norman hunting preserve; most of the Derbyshire countryside was open ground rather than woodland.

The most obvious feature of Chapel-en-le-Frith today is its rather dowdy main road, which sweeps south into a hollow and on towards Buxton. A bypass now carries A6 traffic around to the east, but it will take some years for this part of Chapel to brighten up. However,

turning off the main road at the white-painted Kings Arms at the top of the town, brings you directly to the market place and a change of character. Lovely cobbled paths and a medieval cross and stocks stand at the heart of the little square, overlooked by a café called The Stocks. Except on market day (Thursday) this is a quiet and out of the way place, perfect for a cup of tea and a wander. Close by is the Roebuck Inn, and a little way

77

Insight

PEAK PANTHER

On a bright winter's day in 1995 a small group of birdwatchers saw something out of the ordinary. While wandering by the hedge along the western shores of Combs Reservoir they came across some large clawed footprints measuring 3.5in (89mm) wide, which were sunk deep into the mud. The prints didn't belong to a dog. After studying the photographs they had taken, it became obvious that a huge cat had been on the prowl – probably the infamous Peak Panther that has had may sightings in the hills above Chinley and Hayfield.

14th century by a sturdier structure. Most of what is visible today is from the refurbishment of 1733, but there are hints of antiquity all around; the shaft of a Saxon cross, a weathered sundial, and a view across what must have been glorious hunting country to the scenic crag-fringed edges of Coombs Moss.

The attractive village of Combs, just southwest of Chapel-en-le-Frith, has stone-built cottages centred on the welcoming Beehive Inn. A short walk away is Combs Reservoir, which has a sailing club and is also a popular spot for coarse fishing and birdwatching.

further along the street, opposite the church, is what was once the Bull's Head Inn, of which only the sign, a wooden carved life-size shorthorn bull's head, still survives.

St Thomas à Becket Church stands on a grassy knoll overlooking a housing estate. The original chapel in the forest was built here around 1225, but was replaced in the early

THE GOYT VALLEY

The River Goyt meets the River Tame in Stockport to form the famous River Mersey. Its upper and middle reaches cleave a deep, gorge-like valley through some of the most accessible moorland in the Peak District. This is an area, which is threaded with by-roads, pack-horse trails and old railways tracks.

A place where Cheshire meets Derbyshire amidst a blaze of heather and bilberry-strewn uplands.

The Goyt River flows from south to north; it rises on the slopes of Cat and Fiddle Moor, a wild and windswept place with a reputation for having the worst weather. The moor is named after the Cat and Fiddle Inn, at 1,690ft (515m) it is the second-highest pub in England. Like other high-altitude hostelries, such as The Snake or Tan Hill, it was built in the turnpike era at the start of the 19th century and is still a welcome sight for traffic on the sinuous A537. There are few other buildings to be seen for miles around, but some facilities are available at Derbyshire Bridge, which is the usual starting point to explore the Goyt Valley.

Years ago the Goyt was as natural an upland valley as is possible in England, but the original scatter of ancient oaks has now been augmented or replaced by conifer plantations and the river and meadowlands were flooded to create

Visit

GOYT'S MOSS

Below Cat and Fiddle Moor is Goyt's Moss, a colourful carpet of cotton grass and asphodel belying a treacherous surface of wet peat. In late April and May golden plovers and curlews add their voices to those of pipits and larks; this is also the breeding ground of the twite, a small finch with a pink rump.

the Fernilee and Errwood reservoirs. The combination of lake and forest, cobalt and viridian beneath the magenta of heather moorland, rising to the highest point in Cheshire at nearby Shining Tor, 1,834 feet (559m), makes the Goyt a colourful place; parking and picnic sites around the reservoir shores and walks through the woodlands draw so many walkers and visitors that there is a one-way system up the narrow road to Derbyshire Bridge (further weekend traffic restrictions may be introduced).

LEEK

The little Staffordshire mill town of Leek sits on a broad low hill in a bend of the River Churnet. Unlike most of the other towns circling the Peak District, Leek is not overshadowed by the hills and makes no extravagant claims to be an adventure centre. All around are green valleys and rolling pastures, full of dairy cattle and longwool sheep. To the south lies the Churnet, with a host of visitor attractions, such as the Caldon Canal, the Cheddleton Railway Centre and the old Cheddleton Flint Mill. To the southwest is Stoke-on-Trent with its fine pottery heritage. But to the north and east the foothills rise inexorably to heather moorland and limestone plateaux; like Macclesfield and Glossop there is a sense of a settlement butting as closely to the hills as it dared, exploiting the power of the elements.

Textiles transformed Leek from an old medieval market town to an industrial sprawl, but silk was the speciality, which meant that many of the early mills were small and clean, with better working conditions than those endured in the cotton mills of the Peak valleys. Most of the mill buildings are now put to other uses, but the wealth generated by silk is recalled in the many imposing buildings commissioned from the Victorian architects William and Larner Sugden.

The heart of old Leek, easily missed on a fleeting visit, is the cobbled-stone Market Place. At one end of it stands the 17th-century Butter Cross, a link with the town's dairying tradition. The cross was removed from its original location, at the lower side of the square towards Sheep Market, nearly two hundred years ago and has since been restored. An attractive watermill stands at the edge of the town as a monument to James Brindley, the 18th-century canal engineer. Further upstream, a tributary of the Churnet was dammed to create Rudyard Lake, to supply water for his Trent and Mersey Canal. A few miles north of the town, the Churnet itself has been dammed to form Tittesworth Reservoir, with facilities including a visitor centre, woodland walks, car parks and a bird hide overlooking the shallow northern corner.

Insight

'SCHEMER' BRINDLEY

James Brindley, Leek's most famous son, was actually born at Wormhill, near Tideswell, but his family moved to Leek in 1726 when he was ten years old. He was apprenticed to a millwright at Sutton, near Macclesfield, when he was 17 years old and was soon solving all sorts of engineering problems. Most of his ideas worked, and he was nicknamed 'Schemer'. In 1752, he built his first industrial machine for a coal mine in Clifton. Wealth and notoriety followed, but in his later years he became famous for his canal designs, particularly the Trent and Mersey and its Harecastle Tunnel. Brindley died from pneumonia in 1772.

LYME PARK

Lyme Park (National Trust) on the western edge of the Peak District is a modest mirror image of Chatsworth. The exterior, made grimy by the smoky air of Manchester, is Palladian, the work of Italian architect Giacomo Leoni; it featured in the BBC adaptation of *Pride and Prejudice*. The interior, housing family portraits and a collection of clocks, is Elizabethan but with many additions.

Lyme was the home of the Legh family for 600 years and has sufficient style to make it one of the top visitor attractions in the area. Set in rural gardens, parkland and moorland, yet close Stockport. Those who prefer outdoor attractions to the splendours of the stately home will enjoy the wildfowl on the lake and herds of red and fallow deer among the trees. The 1,300-acre (520ha) park also has excellent short walks and viewpoints: a modest alternative to the high hills if the weather is closing in.

MACCLESFIELD

The town of Macclesfield sits firmly at the foot of the hills, close enough to suffer draughts of frost-laden air and share any low cloud. Specialising in silk was its salvation but also its downfall. From a market town, Macclesfield first became known for buttons, then for all kinds of silken products. By the mid-19th century the town was bursting at the seams, with 56 silk 'throwsters' (producing the thread or thrown silk) and 86 businesses creating silk fabric or finished goods. Despite this success, or perhaps because of it, the workforce lived in wretched conditions, with an appalling level of infant mortality, and with nowhere to go when the industry hit one of its frequent declines.

Silk mills, chapels and banks – solid square buildings of blackened stone – are scattered through the town today. Among them is the huge Sunday School on Roe Street, which is now a heritage centre with a silk museum and shop. Near the old market cross, behind St Michael's Church and its beautiful soot-covered chapel of 1501, lies a narrow garden terrace known as Sparrow Park (officially, the Broadhurst Memorial Gardens). This is a pivot of the old town, a place to stop and ponder its rich and chequered history. Below the gardens there is a steep bank, down which run the picturesque 108 Steps. There is a view through the shrubs of the railway station and over the hinterland of the town, to green remembered foothills at the western face of the Peak.

On the farmland of the foothills, above Sutton Lane Ends and a growing patchwork of housing estates, lie the two Langley Reservoirs. They were built in the mid-19th century to provide clean water for Macclesfield, as a response to infant mortality and disease among the mill workers. But young Charles Tunnicliffe, the famous country artist, knew them in more peaceful times as a haunt of

Activity

TEGG'S NOSE AND THE GRITSTONE TRAIL

The best introduction to the Cheshire slice of the Peak landscape is from Tegg's Nose Country Park, along Buxton Old Road to the east of Macclesfield. There are superb views from the Windy Way car park and walks along a network of tracks and pathways, by the old quarry or down through woodland to the reservoirs above Langley. It is possible at this point to join the Gritstone Trail, a waymarked footpath running the length of Cheshire from Lyme Park to Mow Cop.

sandpipers and moorhens. Further into the hills are Ridgegate and Trentabank reservoirs, the winter resort of pochard and goldeneye; Cheshire's largest heronry is also here. Then comes the conifer blanket of Macclesfield Forest, once part of a vast royal hunting forest.

Close to Trentabank is a Forest Visitor Centre, from where there are walks and drives. At the eastern edge of the forest lies the tiny Chapel of St Stephen, where a rush-bearing ceremony takes place each August. At the highest southern access point there is a path that leads onto open moorland and up to Shutlingsloe, one of the most distinctive of the Peak summits.

About 3 miles (4.8km) south of Macclesfield is Gawsworth Hall, a truly splendid Tudor black-and-white manor house, which was the birthplace of Mary Fitton. This renowned lady is thought by some to be the 'Dark Lady' of Shakespeare's sonnets, who aroused such emotional turmoil in the poet. We shall probably never know, but the house is certainly worth a visit anyway, for its wonderful old timberwork, its paintings and its suits of armour. The grounds, thought to be a rare example of an Elizabethan pleasure garden, include a tilting ground and are the venue for open-air theatre and craft fairs during the summer months.

THE ROACHES

THE ROACHES

There are few real peaks in the Peak District (the name is derived from the Old English pecsaetan, meaning hill-dwellers), but the most elegant and craggy-topped are in the far west: Hen Cloud, Ramshaw Rocks and The Roaches. They are gritstone outcrops, similar to those in the Dark Peak and Eastern Moors, but here they were more heavily contorted or squashed together, leading to a landscape of misfit valleys, steep slopes and rock faces rather than plateau moorland.

The greatest legend associated with the Roaches is the Arthurian tale of *Sir Gawain and the Green Knight*. According to the 14th-century poem a knight on horseback, cloaked entirely in green, gatecrashed a feast at Camelot and challenged the Knights of the Round Table. Sir Gawain rose to the challenge and beheaded the Green Knight but the latter retrieved his head and laughingly challenged Sir Gawain to meet with him again, in

Insight

BEYOND THE LAW

Below Cut-thorn Hill lies Three Shires Head, where a packhorse bridge stands at the cusp between Derbyshire, Cheshire and Staffordshire. Many years ago, this was where illegal prizefights took place because the local police forces had no authority to pursue suspects beyond their own county boundary. For the very same reason, Flash became the capital of coin counterfeiting, and the word Flash ('Flash Harry', 'flash money' etc) entered the language to denote a fake.

a year's time, at the Green Chapel. This has been identified as Lud's Chapel, near the Roaches.

Ramshaw Rocks are probably the best-known outlier of the Roaches, because they tower above the roadside on the A53 north of Leek and have a face-like formation. The A53 and the quiet winding roads to the west of Axe Edge lead to some interesting places.

95

Axe Edge itself is too high to be anything but wild. One notable village tucked away just off the main road is Flash, claimed to be the highest village in England at 1,518 feet (462m). The River Dane rises nearby, jinking a course between hills and ridges and flowing southwest to Gradbach and Danebridge: this is lovely countryside full of trees and meadows, old barns and cowslip banks.

The Roaches ridge lies a few miles to the southwest of Flash and runs northwest – southeast, its main rock-climbing exposures facing the setting sun. A footpath follows the crest of the ridge, linking with Back Forest and creating a 4-mile (6.4km) ridge walk with superb views. Heather clothes the upper hills, bracken and woodland the slopes. If you are walking in the area, look out for Rock Hall bothy built into the rock and containing at least one room that is a natural cave. This listed building is a former gamekeeper's residence, currently owned by the Peak District National Park Authority. Restored in 1989, the Don Whillams Memorial Hut can be booked through the British Mountaineering Council by small groups of climbers.

The area has also become famous as the home of a colony of red-necked wallabies, a Tasmanian oddity that arrived at a private zoo at Swythamley Hall in the 1930s and escaped to form a wild population, although it is a while since there's been a confirmed sighting.

WHALEY BRIDGE

This little town grew up with dust on its face and Goyt water in its veins. Coal and textiles provided the only gainful work – both have now gone. These days there is hardly a whisper of past industry and employment is more varied. Visitors call in on their way to the Goyt Valley or the Peak Forest Canal.

Just outside Whaley Bridge, above Bing Wood (a 'bing' is a slag heap) is the curious scooped-out

THE ROACHES

WILDBOARCLOUGH

ridge known as Roosdyche. This was once described as a Roman racecourse, on purely visual evidence – nobody could explain who or what else could have created such a flat-bottomed valley. The answer, of course, was ice.

South of the town is Toddbrook Reservoir, built to feed the Peak Forest Canal, and tiny Taxal village clustered around its church. Inside St James's are memorials to the Jodrell family, and a monument to Michael Heathcote, 'Gentleman of the Pantry and Yeoman of the Mouth to His Late Majesty King George the Second'. Heathcote lived to be 75 years old, so presumably nobody tried to poison the King during his time as official food-taster.

WILDBOARCLOUGH

Only a few outbuildings remain of the Crag mills that once made this valley hum with the busy sounds of industry and employed more than 600 people. The mills here specialised in bleaching, printing

Insight

WILD COUNTRY

It is difficult to imagine this sweep of country as a dangerous, lonely wilderness, but names on the map like Wolf End and Wildboarclough hint at the reputation that it once enjoyed. This is one of several locations claimed as the place where the last wild boar in England was killed (although nowadays they again forage in the woodlands of Kent, East Sussex and Gloucestershire).

and dyeing of first cotton, then later carpets. However, along the valley today you'll find that most traces of the town's industrial heritage are cleverly camouflaged green. There are shrub-covered foundations, grassy trackways and mossy walls. The stream boasts pretty waterfalls and deep pools and is the territory of dippers and grey wagtails. The impression is of a rural backwater, at the foot of Shutlingsloe, the 'Cheshire Matterhorn'.

TOURST INFORMATION CENTRES

Buxton
The Crescent. Tel: 01298 25106;
www.visitbuxton.co.uk

Leek
Market Place. Tel: 01538 483741;
www.staffsmoorlands.gov.uk

Macclesfield
Council Offices, Town Hall.
Tel: 01625 500500;
www.peaksandplains.co.uk

PLACES OF INTEREST

Brindley Mill
Mill Street, Leek.
Tel: 01538 483741;
www.brindleymill.net

Buxton Museum and Art Gallery
Peak Buildings, Terrace Road
Tel: 01298 24658

Cheddleton Flint Mill
Beside Caldon Canal, Leek Road,
Cheddleton.
Tel: 01782 502907

Cheddleton Railway Centre
Cheddleton Station, Churnet Valley
Railway.
Tel: 01538 360522

Chestnut Centre
Castleton Road, Chapel-en-le-Frith.
Tel: 01298 814099;
www.ottersandowls.co.uk

Otter haven, owl sanctuary.
Hare Hill, 4 miles (6.4km) north of
Macclesfield off B5087.
Tel: 01625 584412

Lyme Park
Disley. Tel: 01663 762023;
www.nationaltrust.org.uk

Macclesfield Silk Heritage
Heritage Centre, Roe Street.
Tel: 01625 613210

Silk Museum & Paradise Mill
Park Lane, Macclesfield.
Tel: 01625 612045;
www.macclesfield.silk.museum

Pavilion Gardens
Buxton. Tel: 01298 23114

Poole's Cavern
Green Lane, Buxton.
Tel: 01298 26978;
www.poolescavern.co.uk.

West Park Museum
West Park, Prestbury Road,
Macclesfield.
Tel: 01625 613210

FOR CHILDREN
Blackbrook Zoological Park
Winkhill, nr Leek. Tel: 01538 308293
Blaze Farm
Wildboarclough.
Tel: 01260 227229; www.blazefarm.com
Freshfields Donkey Sanctuary
Wormhill Road, Peak Forest.
Tel: 01298 79775;
www.donkey-village.org.uk
Rudyard Lake Steam Railway
Tel: 01995 672280;
www.rudyardlake.co.uk

SHOPPING
Buxton
Market, Tue and Sat.
Chapel-en-le-Frith
Market, Thu.
Leek
Market, Wed and Sat.
Macclesfield
Outdoor market, Tue, Fri, Sat.

LOCAL SPECIALITIES
Farmers Markets
Buxton, first Thu.
Leek, third Sat each month.

Spa Water
Spa water from the fountain in
The Crescent, Buxton.

PERFORMING ARTS
Buxton
Opera House, Water Street, Buxton.
Tel: 01298 72190;
www.buxton-opera.co.uk

SPORTS & ACTIVITIES
ANGLING
Fly Fishing
Danebridge Fisheries, Wincle (trout).
Tel: 01260 227293
Errwood Reservoir, Goyt Valley.
Tel: 01663 734220
Lamaload Reservoir, Macclesfield.
Tel: 01625 619935
Coarse
Combs Reservoir, Whaley Bridge.
Tel: 01663 762393
Rudyard Lake.
Tel: 01538 306280;
www.rudyardlake.co.uk

BOAT HIRE/SAILING
Rudyard Lake
Tel: 01538 306280
COUNTRY PARKS AND NATURE RESERVES
Grinlow and Buxton Country Park.
Tegg's Nose Country Park,
Macclesfield.
Tel: 01625 614278
Tittesworth Reservoir.
Tel: 01538 300400
CYCLING
Macclesfield Forest
On and off-road routes.
Rudyard Lake, near Leek
Level cycling trail on old railway
beside Rudyard Lake.
The Middlewood Way
Runs northwards from Macclesfield
to Marple.
CYCLE HIRE
Parsley Hay
Parsley Hay Bike Hire.
Tel: 01298 84493
Whaley Bridge
The Bike Factory, 3 Market Street.
Tel: 01663 735020

GUIDED WALKS
Professional Blue Badge Guides.
Tel: 01629 534284
Buxton
From Tourist Information Centre.
Tel: 01298 25106
Etherow–Goyt Walks.
Etherow Country Park.
Tel: 01614 276937
Leek
Town walks from Leek Tourist
Information Centre.
Tel: 01538 483741
Peak District
Annual Peak District Walking Festival.
Guided walks.
Tel: 0870 444 7275;
www.visitpeakdistrict.com/walk
Walking the Bollin Valley
The Bollin Valley Project Office.
Tel: 01625 534790
National Park Walks with a Ranger
Peak District National Park.
Tel: 01629 816200;
www.peakdistrict.org.uk

HANG GLIDING
Leek
Peak Hang Gliding Centre, York House,
Ladderedge, Leek.
Tel: 07000 426445;
www.peakhanggliding.co.uk

HORSE-RIDING
Buxton
Buxton Riding Centre, Fern Farm.
Tel: 01298 72319

Flash
Northfield Farm Riding & Trekking
Centre, Flash.
Tel: 01298 22543

**LONG-DISTANCE
FOOTPATHS & TRAILS**
The Gritstone Trail
35 miles (56km) from Disley in
Cheshire to Kidsgrove in Staffordshire.

The Middlewood Way
11-mile (18km) trail between
Macclesfield and Marple.

The Midshires Way
230 miles (363km) from Stockport to
Buckinghamshire.

The Monsal Trail
8.5 miles (13.7km) from Blackwell Mill
Junction to Coomb's Viaduct.

The Pennine Bridleway
350 miles (560km) from Cromford to
Byrness (Northumberland).

ANNUAL EVENTS & CUSTOMS
For the full programme visit
www.visitpeakdistrict.com
Well dressing in Chapel-en-le-Frith,
Buxworth and Buxton, Jul.

Buxton
Antiques Fair, May.
Buxton Festival, Jul.
Buxton Fringe Festival, Jul.
International Gilbert & Sullivan
Festival, Jul/Aug.
Country Music Festival, Sep.

Cheddleton
Carnival, Aug.

Flash
Teapot Parade, Jun.

Leek
Leek Arts Festival and Carnival, May.
Leek & District Show, Jul.

Macclesfield
Sheep Dog Trials, Aug.

Macclesfield Forest
Rush-bearing ceremony, St Stephen's
Church, Aug.

105

TEA ROOMS

Brookside Café
Wildboarclough, Macclesfield,
Cheshire, SK11 0BD
Tel: 01260 227632

Something of an institution amongst
ramblers and cyclists in this corner of
the Peak District, the Brookside has
been offering sustenance for more than
40 years. Expect great home-cooking,
from afternoon teas to tasty meals,
served amidst stunning countryside.

The Coffee Shop
Lyme Park, Disley,
Cheshire, SK12 2NX
Tel: 01663 762023

In the shadow of the superb Lyme Hall,
this unpretentious and welcoming
place offers simple, filling fare. There's
a more extensive restaurant in the
grand surroundings of Lyme Hall itself.

Roaches Tea Room
Paddock Farm, Upper Hulme,
Leek, Staffordshire, ST13 5SE
Tel: 01538 300345

A very homely place at which to indulge
in that local delicacy, the Staffordshire
oatcake (a dream with bacon and
cheese), cream teas, calorific treats or
maybe just a mug of tea, enjoying the
remarkable scenery of The Roaches.
The friendly folk at Paddock Farm cater
for walkers and climbers.

The Coffee Tavern
Shrigley Road, Pott Shrigley,
Bollington, Cheshire, SK10 5SE
Tel: 01625 576370

This is a firm favourite with walkers,
cyclists and diners in these western
fringes of the Peak District Here you
can enjoy anything from a modest pot
of tea and a cake or a light snack to a
full-blown three-course meal.

BUXTON

The Swan Inn

Macclesfield Road, Kettleshulme,
Whaley Bridge, Cheshire, SK23 7QU
Tel: 01663 732943; www.the-swan-
inn-kettleshulme.co.uk

Rescued from closure by a consortium
of villagers, this tiny pub is a champion
of local brewery beers, complementing
the range of largely locally sourced
food. It's the perfect place to unwind
after a good walk.

The Ship Inn

Wincle, Cheshire, SK11 0QE
Tel: 01260 227217

This pub clings to the steep side of the
Dane Valley above superb woodlands
and the enticing ridges and clefts
of the western Peak. Just two little
rooms shelter happy drinkers of local
beers and contented diners feasting
on a superb menu strong on excellent
Cheshire produce.

Quiet Woman

Earl Sterndale, Buxton,
Derbyshire, SK17 9SL
Tel: 01298 83211

No music here, just the hum of
conversation over home-made pork
pies washed down with Marstons and a
couple of guest beers. Behind the pub
is a smallholding with friendly stock to
keep the children entertained.

The Hanging Gate

Meg Lane, Higher Sutton,
Macclesfield, Cheshire, SK11 0NG
Tel: 01260 252238

Blazing open fires, gnarled beams,
country-cottage décor, exemplary
food, beers from Hydes brewery; it's
a mixture made in heaven, popular
with ramblers and birdwatchers using
Macclesfield Forest.

White Peak

ASHFORD IN THE WATER

BAKEWELL

EYAM

HADDON HALL

LATHKILL DALE

MILLER'S DALE

PEAK FOREST

STANTON IN PEAK

TIDESWELL

WINSTER

YOULGREAVE

INTRODUCTION

Bakewell is the mid-point of the Peak District and through it runs the River Wye: downstream is the fine medieval mansion, Haddon Hall. Upstream the river quickens as the valley narrows surrounded by limestone hills. Little side valleys twist their way through the fossil seabed. Water often flows far below the ground, so that in past centuries village folk relied on wells, and gave thanks each summer for their constancy. The White Peak is a land of drystone walls and beautiful dales, of crouched churches and good pubs.

Unmissable attractions

Take your pick from 1,600 miles (2,560km) of public footpaths crossing wild moor, beside river banks and past sleepy villages for a walk...cycle along the Tissington, High Peak and Monsal trails: former railway lines now converted to leisure routes for walkers and cyclists...taste the famous pudding at Bakewell...explore the romantic medieval pile of Haddon Hall, frequently used as a film location...take a wander around the most attractive of all the Peak villages, Ashford in the Water...ponder the ancient purpose of Arbor Low at Youlgreave, a famous henge built by the Beaker People.

1

1 Monsal Dale
A narrow footbridge spans the waters of the River Wye in Monsal Dale. Stop off at Monsal Head, above the valley (there is a large car park) to admire the far-reaching views of the dale and the river down below.

2 Ashford in the Water
Nestling on the banks of the River Wye, Ashford in the Water is one of the most attractive of the Peak villages. It is well known for its colourful Blessing of the Wells procession, which takes place annually on Trinity Sunday.

3 Bakewell
The original Bakewell Pudding was the result of a culinary error. However, the recipe was such a success that a Mrs Wilson, wife of the local Tallow Chandler, started making the puddings for sale from this location in Bakewell from 1860 onwards.

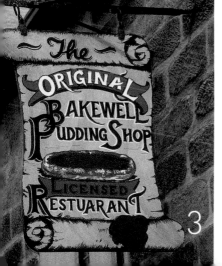

ASHFORD IN THE WATER

Only 2 miles (3.2km) from Bakewell, just off the busy A6, it is a wonder that Ashford in the Water has kept any kind of dignity. In fact it is one of the most attractive and interesting of all the Peak villages, sited on a twist of the River Wye, on the ancient port but bypassed by the new road.

Grassland and the A6 have taken the place of the 'black marble' quarry works on the approach to the village. 'Black marble' was an impure limestone that turned shiny black when polished; it was popular in Victorian times (for vases, fire-surrounds, etc) and the works were extensive and probably represented the only blot on the Ashford horizon. This is not to say there had not been industry in the village before Henry Watson established his marble works in 1748. It simply means the scale was different. Many of the wonderful stone houses and cottages on the main triangle of lanes served as workshops when they were built; there was a corn mill, a candle-maker and several stocking mills. The community was more varied and the buildings more eccentric, and this has left a distinctive character to the place today, part pretty English village, part quirky Derbyshire jumble.

At the middle of Ashford is a green space, called Hall Orchard, once part of the grounds of Neville Hall, a medieval hunting lodge that stood on the eastern side. It is now a playing field but there are some tall trees, notably limes, and around the rest of the village fine ash trees offer shelter and shade. 'Oak won't grow in Ashford' goes the local saying, and this has proved true over the years.

On Church Street, between the Hall Orchard and the Wye, is a 17th-century tithe barn (a private house) and the parish church. Most of the structure of the church is Victorian but just above the porch, returned to its original position, is a Norman tympanum. The Normans were not as expert as the Saxons at carving animals so there is some doubt

Visit

VIRGIN CROWNS

In Ashford church hang four 18th-century virgin crants, or crowns. These were funeral garlands, carried at maidens' funerals and then hung on beams or from the roof of the church. They are made of white paper attached to a wicker frame, and in the middle is a paper glove, bearing the name of the girl. The tradition of virgin crowns was widespread across England, but rarely do any of the fragile garlands survive to tell the sad tale.

about what the stone slab depicts. It may be a tree of life with a boar on one side and a lion on the other, or it may be meant to represent the Royal Forest with a boar and a wolf.

The main attraction for visitors to Ashford is the river, crystal clear and full of trout. There is space to wander along the banks, and three bridges, of which two are old. Close to the cricket field the bridge on the closed road carries an inscription 'M. Hyde 1664'; the brief memorial refers to The Reverend Hyde, who was thrown from his horse and drowned in the river below. Upstream, on an old packhorse trail, is the attractive Sheepwash Bridge; a stone fold on one side shows where the sheep were held before being plunged into the river and made to swim across.

Southwest of Ashford, on the dry-limestone plateau, is Sheldon, a small lead-mining village close to the famous Magpie Mine. The main shaft of the mine was 728 feet (222m) deep and water had to be pumped up to a sough, which carried it to the Wye on the curve below Great Shacklow Wood. In 1966 the roof of the sough collapsed and there was an explosion of pent-up mud and rocks. The resulting debris can still be seen today; the floodwater was gone all too quickly in a tidal wave.

Ashford has grown used to being flooded – 'in the Water' was added to the name quite recently.

BAKEWELL

THE SECRET

UR SECRET

LOUNGE LIZARD

BAKEWELL

Bakewell is always busy with visitors and locals. Its streets are never free of traffic and bustle, but if you accept this from the outset there's every reason to enjoy the town; it is a tourist honeypot that is still serves as a working community.

There are a surprisingly few very old buildings considering the rich history of Bakewell (it was granted a market and 15-day fair in 1254), but there are a number of 17th-century structures, such as the Market Hall, which serves as the Peak District National Park Information Centre, and the Town Hall. Up the steep road on the west side of the town stands an airy grass-covered knoll on which sits the parish church of All Saints. Like many of the churches in Derbyshire it is broad and low, but with a spire as sharp as a 3H pencil. Inside you will find some fragments of Saxon and Norman stonework, and the famous monument to Sir John Manners and his wife Dorothy, who are reputed to have eloped

Insight

BAKEWELL PUDDING

The fame of the humble Bakewell Pudding has spread so far that it is now high on the list of favourite British puddings. According to tradition, the recipe was the result of an error that emanated from the kitchen of the Rutland Arms Hotel in around 1860. The cook, flustered perhaps by a special order to prepare a strawberry tart for some very important guests, put the jam in first, then poured in the egg mixture designed for the pastry on top. Far from being a disaster, the new invention was hailed as a culinary triumph and became a regular item on the menu. Incidentally, don't ask for a Bakewell Tart in the home of their origin – they are always known here as 'puddings'. And please don't enquire who owns the original recipe, included in the will of the cook at the Rutland Arms – it is still the cause of local dispute and rivalry!

Visit

TROUT WATCHING

One of the idlest pleasures on rivers like the Wye is to stand on a bridge and watch trout keeping stationary against the current below. Swimming against the flow looks remarkably easy, if you have the fins for it. Brown trout, with spotted flanks, are the native game fish made famous by *The Compleat Angler*; the rainbow trout is an American import, able to tolerate warmer and more polluted water.

together from Haddon Hall in 1558. Outside the hall stands the shaft of a 9th-century stone cross, decorated with vine scrolls and figures. Nearby to the church is The Old House and Cunningham Place, a fine 16th-century parsonage now a museum.

Monday is market day, when cattle and sheep wagons converge behind Bridge Street and the market place is decked with awnings. Escaping the bleating and banter is very easy; the River Wye runs alongside, and within a few seconds it is possible to be out of the crowd and feeding ducks or trout along the river. Upstream is one of the oldest bridges in England, built in about 1300; impossible to appreciate if you are driving over it but a scene-stealer from water level where its five arches and solid breakwaters are visible. In the distance stands Castle Hill, where the settlement of Bakewell began in 920 AD with the establishment of a Mercian fort.

EYAM

Disease and suffering was an ievitable part of life in medieval England, and many of the Peak villages suffered from the plague. What made the weaving village of Eyam special was the attempt by the local rector, William Mompesson, to keep the outbreak in 1665–66 within the confines of the community. The village was put in quarantine, entire families perished and Eyam became a byword for tragedy and self-sacrifice.

EYAM

Insight & Visit

GEOLOGY OF THE PLAGUE VILLAGE

Exploring the upper pathways of the village, such as the grassy alley from the Royal Oak up Little Edge and along May Walk, it is obvious that Eyam lies on the very edge of the limestone and only just qualifies as a White Peak village. In fact, most of the houses sited on the north side, towards Eyam Edge, were constructed using sandstone, which was the preferred building material, whilst the greyer, less durable limestone was used a few hundred yards away to the south. Just across the valley, and – perhaps understandably – rarely mentioned in tourist guidebooks, you can see two great working quarries, ripping into the hills for road stone.

According to tradition, the plague virus was introduced into the village by a tailor called George Viccars, who bought some infected cloth from London. He died a few days after arriving at Eyam, lodging with Mary Cooper at what is now called Plague Cottage. A fortnight later Mary's son Edward died and the whole community braced itself for disaster. The young rector quickly sent his children away, but stayed with his wife to care for the sick and organise the quarantine. Over the months, through 1665 and into the autumn of 1666, about 250 people died, including Mompesson's wife, but the heroic efforts of the village were successful and the epidemic did not spread outside Eyam.

Some of the story has been embellished, but the details are recorded in the parish register, among the gravestones around St Lawrence's Church and on nearby cottages. Towns such as Derby and Chesterfield probably suffered worse epidemics of bubonic plague; Eyam has kept its unique place in history because you can stand beside victims' homes, read about their lives and look across to their graves.

Eyam today is neither a sad place nor dwelling in the past. It stands on the hill brow between

Insight & Visit

HERALDIC BEASTS

Important and aristocratic families always had their own ancestral emblems or devices, which accounts for the curious animal shapes that appear on the gutters and in the ironwork of Haddon Hall. The boar emblem represents the Vernon family and the peacock the Manners family; they appear together all over the estate, most spectacularly as carefully clipped and maintained topiary figures in the huge yew bushes outside the gardener's cottage.

Middleton Dale and Eyam Moor, as self-contained and aloof as ever. Visitors are impressed by the Saxon cross in St Lawrence's churchyard and come to enjoy the traditional well dressing and the sheep roast. But folk-memories of the plague still send a shiver down the spine.

HADDON HALL

Close your eyes and imagine a rambling castle, built with style, English to the core, unchanged for centuries, full of ghosts, set among trees and pastures above a clear meandering river. What you have in mind is Haddon Hall. It is the most impressive and authentic building in the Peak District, the one that turns historians into poets and is a firm favourite with film-makers. The hall featured in *Pride and Prejudice* (2005) starring Keira Knightly, Matthew MacFadeyn and Dame Judy Dench. Why is this? It's simple. It is a perfectly proportioned medieval manor house, hardly touched since the 16th century.

Haddon Hall was originally owned by the Vernon family from 1170 until 1567; it came to them by marriage and passed to the Manners family in the same way. Over all those years the house was extended gradually; the Peveril Tower in the 12th century, the cross-wing in the 14th, battlements in the 15th, a gatehouse and courtyard in the 16th and the Long Gallery early in the 17th century. But after that Haddon

HADDON HALL

Hall was left to slumber while the Manners family moved to Belvoir Castle as Dukes of Rutland.

Thus the house escaped the fickle architectural fashions of the 18th and 19th centuries, but it was not neglected – it was meticulously maintained, so that when the 9th Duke (then the Marquis of Granby) began his restoration in the early 20th century, his task was by no means daunting. The duke ensured that as much as possible of the original structure should be preserved, and that any replacements were carried out to the highest standards. Today Haddon Hall reflects a sense of history that only comes from remaining in the same family for over 800 years.

LATHKILL DALE

The classic farmscape is dramtically disrupted on the White Peak plateau by the Derbyshire Dales, a series of steep-sided valleys in the limestone. These dales form a National Nature Reserve, and the jewel is Lathkill, which runs eastwards from Monyash to the River Wye below Haddon. Access to Lathkill Dale is from Monyash or Over Haddon, 2 miles (3.2km) southwest of Bakewell.

From the west the dale starts out dry, but between Ricklow and Cales Dale the River Lathkill rises out of a cave and soon broadens out into a crystal-clear stream, the haunt of water voles and dippers.

Unlike the pasture and silage fields of the plateau, the grassland of the dale is ablaze with wild flowers. The rabbit-cropped south-facing slopes sparkle with rockrose and trefoil, which attract blue butterflies and burnet and forester moths. The shaded herbage of the north-facing slopes is the habitat for one of the Dales' specialities, Jacob's ladder. Further down the Lathkill, following the well-worn footpath towards Over Haddon, grassland gives way to scrub and to ash woodland that, in the early summer casts a translucent shade and is full of songbirds.

Lathkill Dale looks untouched, but for many centuries it was mined for lead. The shafts, drainage channels and spoil-heaps have been absorbed into the landscape that they enhance its beauty. Most of the lead was exhausted by the 18th century but in the 1840s there was an attempt to drain the deep mines by building a steam engine, powered by a huge waterwheel fed by the Mandale viaduct. The scheme was a disaster, as was the Over Haddon gold rush of 1894.

MILLER'S DALE

The River Wye rises at Buxton then flows east to dissect the limestone plateau. Each reach of the river has its own character, and each section of the narrow valley or dale has its own name. Thus Wye Dale turns into Chee Dale, which gives way to Miller's Dale, then Water-cum-Jolly Dale and Monsal Dale.

The presence of the river is a unifying theme; it brought welcome industry to the outback in the days of the Industrial Revolution and around this industry the little settlement of Miller's Dale grew up, squeezed awkwardly into the narrow valley of the Wye. Here lived the rail men and quarry workers and there was even a station, but all of that is gone now and the industrial areas are returning to nature.

In many respects Miller's Dale, to either side of Litton Mill, is the most impressive dale to visit. Not only does the Wye negotiate a barrage of natural obstacles here, side-stepping hills, twisting through gaps and gorges and rock faces, but there are mill races and weirs where the power of the water has been diverted to drive 19th-century cotton mills (Litton and Cressbrook, a little way further downstream). A recreational footpath, the Monsal Trail, runs the length of the dale, allowing access to the old mill yards (some of the buildings are still in use, but not for weaving). There are footbridges at either end of Miller's Dale allowing access to car parks.

PEAK FOREST

Several side dales run north from the main valley, often dry and grassy but sometimes decked with beautiful ash woodland and with a stream. The most attractive are Cressbrook Dale, the best for wildlife and with ash woodland, Tideswell Dale, with access to Tideswell village, and Monks Dale, close to Wormhill. Wormhill belies its name by being an attractive scatter of old farmhouses, with a village green, stocks and a fountain/well (dressed in August) commemorating James Brindley, the famous canal engineer, who was born close by at Tunstead.

PEAK FOREST

High, wide and windswept, it's hard to believe that this was once a royal chase – the Forest in the Peak – or that its administrative capital was this little village. For about a century, until the relaxation of the Forest Laws in 1250, kings and princes used the expanse of woodland and heath between the Goyt and the Derwent rivers as a private playground; they hunted wild boar and roe deer and stayed at the recently built Peveril Castle, which stands high above Castleton.

By Elizabethan times most of the ancient woodland had disappeared, but what remained of the wilderness was fenced in as a deer park. A Steward and five Royal Foresters managed the enclosure system and had premises in the Chamber, a building on the site of the present Chamber Farm. Swainmotes, or forest courts, settled any disputes. It was the foresters' task to care for the deer, by controlling grazing, by preventing walls from being built and by keeping people out. The deer increased fourfold, but this was only a temporary triumph. Around 1655 the land was allocated to the Dukes of Devonshire and was officially deforested, though the last of the trees had already been felled to provide pit props for the coal mines on Coombs Moss. Scrub and heath took over the countryside until the turn of the 19th century.

Activity

WYE VALLEY VIEWPOINT

Pilhough Lane, going northeast out of Stanton, makes a pleasant walk or drive because of its panoramic views over the Wye Valley and Haddon Hall. Before the church was built parishioners had to walk this way to Rowsley, and the Thornhill family had a viewing platform, called the Stand or Belvedere, set into the steep edge so that people could stop, rest and enjoy the fine prospect before them.

The Chamber of the Peak, and the few cottages that made up the village of Peak Forest, had been the heart of the royal forest, but had not stood among trees; this part of the limestone plateau was called the Great Pasture and was used for grazing sheep, as it is now. The present village of stone-built houses and farms grew up around a church built by the Dowager Duchess of Devonshire when the land was first acquired. This was at the time of the Commonwealth and could only be construed as an act of defiance when considering its dedication – to 'King Charles, King and Martyr'.

STANTON IN PEAK

Important ritual landscapes, stretches of countryside, which were set aside in prehistoric times because of their spiritual significance, are not confined to Stonehenge and the Dorset Cercus. Apart from megaliths and barrows, such places often retain traces of avenues and earth banks, dykes and cairns. They draw the eye from miles around, dominating the high ground and casting a palpable send of magic on everyone from archaeologists to New Age travellers. They ask so many questions of our modern culture that they are as uncomfortable as they are fascinating. Such a place is ancient Stanton Moor.

Stanton village is a ribbon of cottages on a steep and winding side road, built out of the limestone

MOCK BEGGAR'S WALL

TIDESWELL

TIDESWELL

and below the brow of the gritstone, sheltered from the moor by old quarries and a swathe of tall sweet-chestnut trees. The initials WPT, carved into the lintels of many doorways, refer to William Thornhill, who built most of the village in the 1830s and whose family lived at Stanton Hall. The 18th-century Flying Childers Inn celebrates the greatest racehorse of its day, trained by Sir Hugh Childers for the 4th Duke of Devonshire. Opposite the inn is Holly House that still has half of its windows still blocked up to avoid the 1697 window tax.

Birchover Lane, running south of Stanton, follows the western edge of the moor. Parking places give access to pathways through birch scrub and over heather and bilberry to the Bronze Age landscape. About 70 barrows or burial cairns have been identified on the small island of gritstone. The biggest, covering the site of twelve cremations, still stands 5 feet (1.5m) tall, inside a double ring of stones with an outer diameter

Visit

ROCKING STONES

Many of the sandstone outcrops that rise out of the bracken between Stanton and Elton have historical associations. Rowtor Rocks, near Birchover and overlooking the Druid Inn, was famous for its Rocking Stones, but the best of these is a 50-ton block on a sandstone pivot. Unfortunately, it was vandalised in 1799 and no longer moves. At the foot of nearby Cratcliff Rocks is a hermit's cave, once the abode of a rabbit-catcher.

of 54 feet (16.4m). There are three stone circles or monuments on Stanton Moor, the most famous is the Nine Ladies. Outside this stone ring, about 100 feet (30.5m) to the south, stands the solitary King Stone, which is part of the ritual site. The story goes that a fiddler and nine maidens were turned to stone for dancing on Sunday. This is a typical example of prehistoric pagan culture being Christianised.

141

Insight

TIDESWELL CROSSES

In the 15th century all the roads around Tideswell were marked by stone crosses. Unfortunately, only one of these survives intact, at Wheston to the west, close to the 17th-century hall; the rest just exist in fragments, their water-filled bases built into walls and gateposts. A local tradition is to float a cross made of grass blades on the water and make a wish.

TIDESWELL

Daniel Defoe, searching for the famous 'Seven Wonders of the Peak' in 1726, was not impressed by the ebbing and flowing well he viewed in a garden of Manchester Road in Tideswell. This may have been because he was looking at the wrong well (the original 'Wonder' was probably at Barmoor Clough), but in any case the water no longer ebbs and flows with the tide, and Tideswell got its name from an ancient British chieftain called Tidi.

This is not to say that wells were not important in the village; it lies at the 1,000-foot (304m) contour on the limestone plateau, set in a dry bowl amid a grey cobwebbing of walls and wind-scorched fields. In fact, Tideswell is renowned for the quality of its well-dressing ceremony, which starts the Wakes Week on the Saturday nearest Saint John the Baptist's Day (24 June); the week's festivities are concluded with a traditional torchlight procession and a unique Morris Dance.

In the 14th century Tideswell was a thriving, prosperous place, confident in the future of the wool trade and lead mining. The parish church, dedicated to Saint John the Baptist, reflected this optimism; it was built in just 75 years and was a classic cruciform shape, of Decorated and Perpendicular styles, spacious and with superb fittings, carvings and brasses. That Tideswell dwindled to a be just a village was in some ways a stroke of luck, particularly as the glorious church,

TIDESWELL

Insight

THE SEVEN WONDERS OF THE PEAK

The 'Seven Wonders of the Peak' first appeared in print in 1622 in a set of poems by Michael Drayton. His list included Peak Cavern, Poole's Cavern, Eldon Hole, St Ann's Well, the ebbing and flowing well at Tideswell, Mam Tor and Peak Forest. Some years later Thomas Hobbes wrote a poem also including Seven Wonders, but substituting Chatsworth House for Peak Forest. It was left to the redoubtable traveller, Daniel Defoe, in his Tour of 1726, to debunk the myth of the wonders – including the singularly unimpressive well at Tideswell.

often described as the 'Cathedral of the Peak', was bypassed by rich patrons and Victorian megalomaniacs, and stands today in splendid unaltered isolation. Around the church, the largest in the area, run lawns and railings separating it from the more prosaic buildings at the heart of the village.

Two of Tideswell's renown musical forefathers are buried in the church: 'the Minstrel of the Peak', William Newton, who died in 1830, and Samuel Slack, who died in 1822. Slack, whose name bore no relation to his vocal chords, was famous for two things: singing for George III and for stopping a bull dead in its tracks by bellowing at it. His mighty voice, apparently, could be heard a mile (1.6km) away.

To the east of Tideswell is the little village of Litton, a pretty gathering of 18th-century cottages beside a green with a set of stocks close to the Red Lion pub. Tideswell Dale and Cressbrook Dale run south, from west and east of the village, beautiful in their own right and giving access to Miller's Dale.

WINSTER

Midway between the sleepy little villages of Elton and Wensley (which has its own Wensley Dale, but without the cheese) rests the sleepy little village of Winster. People go to Winster because they intend to as it lies off the main tourist routes, though close enough to Matlock to make use of its shops and services. Most of the attraction of Winster is its characterful history, as one of the old lead-mining centres with 18th-century houses lining the main street between a fine 17th-century Dower House and a 15th- to 16th-century Market House. The latter is matchbox-sized and a delightful structure of weathered stone arches, once open but now bricked in to keep it all standing, and an upper floor of brick, which may have replaced its earlier timbers. The Market House was bought by the National Trust in 1906, its first acquisition in the Peaks, and part of it houses an Information Centre. Close by is Winster Hall, an early Georgian house, now a hotel said to be haunted.

Winster used to be full of alehouses; witness the name Shoulder of Mutton, carved by the door of what is now a private house

Activity

A HERMIT'S CAVE NEAR ELTON

West of Winster is the old lead-mining village of Elton. A popular walk heading north from the village leads to a small medieval hermit's cave at Cratcliffe Rocks – carved into the cave is a crucifix. An unusual rock formation known as Robin Hood's Stride and a stone circle are also seen on this walk of about 4 miles (6.4km).

Visit

CRESSBROOK DALE

Cressbrook Dale, just to the south of Tideswell, is part of the Derbyshire Dales National Nature Reserve. There's plenty of flora and fauna to admire. You may see wild orchids, cranesbill, mountain pansy, globeflower and spring sandwort growing on the limestone grassland in abundance. One of the many alkaline-loving plants is the Nottingham catchfly, which loves dry, stony places. The white flowers roll back in daytime, but are fragrant at night. Small insects are often caught on the sticky stalks to be devoured later by the plant.

NINE LADIES

Visit

ARBOR LOW'S ANCIENT STONES

Three miles (4.8km) along the Long Rake west of Youlgreave, off the road to the left and accessible from a car park, is the famous henge of Arbor Low, probably built by the Beaker People in around 2,000 BC. The whole monument, with rock-cut ditch, bank and a circle of 47 stones, measures 250 feet (76.2m) across. Although the massive stone blocks are all lying flat and half buried, Arbor Low is still a powerful place, especially in winter sunlight.

A more recent tradition is that of pancake races on Shrove Tuesday. It began as harmless, light-hearted fun, organised by the local headmaster as a diversion during wartime for the children, but has now become a more serious – but still fun – affair, with secret race training and stringent rules about making the batter.

YOULGREAVE

A long, handsome village on the shoulder of Bradford Dale, Youlgreave (known as Pommie by most locals) has one of the most elaborate well-dressing ceremonies in the Peak District, taking place at Midsummer each year, when five wells are dressed with biblical scenes. The White Peak tradition has its roots in the days when wells were essential and were blessed to give thanks for water. However, in the case of Youlgreave the records only go back to 1829, coinciding with the provision of the village's own public water supply via a conduit from the

on West Bank. At the top of the bank, just out of the village, is the still-thriving Miners Standard, which has on display some of the fascinating old lead-mining equipment. It is here that the traditional Winster Morris perform their lively dances at the start of Wakes Week in June each year; a procession then leads all the way through the village, finishing up at the Miners Standard for refreshment.

Dale below. The water was gathered in a huge circular stone tank called The Fountain, which stands in the middle of the village. Nearby, on the opposite side of the street, is the Co-op building, which once had a vital role in the social survival of the area but is now a youth hostel.

On the east side of Youlgreave, by the road which then sweeps down to Alport, stands All Saints Church, described by experts as one of the most impressive churches in Derbyshire. Essentially Norman and with an unusually broad nave, the most obvious feature of All Saints is its 14th-century tower, chunky and stylish in the best Perpendicular tradition. Inside are sturdy columns and a 13th-century font, unique in that it has two bowls, and the fine monuments include a tiny effigy of Thomas Cokayne, who died in 1488. The church was restored in 1870 and has stained-glass windows by Burne-Jones and Kempe.

Three bridges cross the River Bradford below Youlgreave, including

Insight

DEW PONDS
Dew ponds are a feature of limestone pastures in the White Peak. Because the underlying rock is porous there are no natural pools, so farmers have created their own. The ponds are named after a famous pond-maker, Mr Dew.

a clapper bridge of stone slabs and a packhorse bridge, which is now used as a footbridge. The short walk to the confluence with the Lathkill is popular, but by turning southeast, over the main bridge and on to the Limestone Way, you can explore the fine countryside towards Birchover, past the Iron Age hill fort of Castle Hill and the Nine Rings Stone Circle (four stones are still standing), to the tumbling rock tors of Robin Hood's Stride (once known as Mock Beggars Hall), Cratcliffe Rocks and Rowtor Rocks. Pagan myths, hermits' caves and a popular pub, the Druid Inn, are among its many attractions.

WHITE PEAK

TOURIST INFORMATION CENTRE
Bakewell
The Old Market Hall,
Bridge Street.
Tel: 01629 813227

PLACES OF INTEREST
Arbor Low Stone Circle
Upper Oldhams Farm, Monyash.
Eyam Hall
Tel: 01433 631976;
www.eyamhall.com
The furniture, portraits and other items at the Hall reflect the fact that this is still a family home and has been for centuries. Also home to a craft centre.
Eyam Museum
Tel: 01433 631371;
www.eyammuseum.demon.co.uk
The museum tells the story of the bubonic plague, how it reached Eyam and was contained there.

Haddon Hall
Bakewell.
Tel: 01629 812855;
www.haddonhall.co.uk
A splendid house that has remained virtually untouched by the passage of time. Topiary gardens.
Old House Museum
Bakewell.
Tel: 01629 813642;
www.oldhousemuseum.org.uk
This Tudor house is home to a folk museum and a Victorian kitchen; toys and lace are among the exhibits.
Winster Market House
Winster, 4 miles (6.4km) west of Matlock.
Tel: 01335 350503
Restored by the National Trust, the Market House is now used as an information centre. The building dates back to the late 17th/early 18th century.

SHOPPING
Bakewell
Market on Mon, includes cattle, except Bank Holidays Mons when a general market is held.

LOCAL SPECIALITIES
Bakewell Puddings
Original Bakewell Pudding Shop,
The Square, Bakewell.
Tel: 01629 812193;
www.bakewellpuddingshop.co.uk
Bloomers Original Bakewell Puddings,
Water Lane, Bakewell.
Tel: 01629 814844
General Foodstuffs
Farmers Market, last Sat of the month,
Bakewell.
Foods from the Chatsworth Estate,
Chatsworth Farm Shop, Stud Farm,
Pilsley, Bakewell.
Tel: 01246 583392

Meats
New Close Farm Shop, Over Haddon,
Bakewell.
Tel: 01629 814280
Home cured pork, bacon and cooked meats.
Pork Pies
Connoisseurs Deli,
Water Street, Water Lane, Bakewell.
Tel: 01629 812044

SPORTS & ACTIVITIES
GUIDED WALKS
Bakewell & Peak District

Professional Blue Badge Guides can arrange walks for individuals or for parties of walkers.
Tel: 01629 534284.

Derbyshire Dales Countryside Service

Planning and Development Services, Town Hall, Matlock. Full guided walks service. Tel: 01629 761326 for details.

National Park Walks with a Ranger

For more details contact the Peak District National Park
Tel: 01629 816200;
www.peakdistrict.org.uk

Peak District

Annual Peak District Walking Festival. Large programme of guided walks held in late Apr/early May.
Tel: 0870 444 7275;
www.visitpeakdistrict.com/walk

HANG GLIDING
Bradwell

Derbyshire Flying Centre.
Tel: 01298 872313;
www.d-f-c.co.uk

HORSE-RIDING
Haddon House Riding Stables

Over Haddon, Bakewell.
Tel: 01629 813723;
www.haddonhousestables.co.uk

LONG-DISTANCE
FOOTPATHS & TRAILS
The Monsal Trail

Runs for 8.5 miles (13.7km) from Blackwell Mill Junction near Buxton to Coombs Viaduct near Bakewell.

The Limestone Way

A 46-mile (74km) route south from Castleton through the White Peak to Rocester (Staffordshire).

ANNUAL EVENTS & CUSTOMS

For the full programme visit
www.visitpeakdistrict.com

Ashford in the Water
Well dressing, late May–early Jun.
Blessing of the Wells Trinity Sunday,
May.

Bakewell
Well dressing, late Jun/early Jul.
Carnival, early Jul.
Bakewell Show, early Aug.

Bradwell
Well dressing, early Aug.

Eyam
Well dressing and demonstration, Aug.
Plague Commemoration Service,
last Sunday in Aug.
Carnival, Aug/Sep.

Flagg
Point-to-Point races, first Tue
after Easter.

Little Longstone
Well-dressing and demonstration,
mid-Jul.

Litton
Well-dressing demonstration, mid-Jun.
Well-dressing, late Jun/early Jul.
Litton Horticultural Show, early Sep.

Middleton by Youlgreave
Well-dressing demonstration, late May.
Well-dressing, late May/early Jun.

Monyash
Well-dressing demonstration, late May.
Well-dressing, late May/early Jun.
Antiques and Collectors' Fair, late Aug.

Pilsley
Well dressing, mid to late Jul.

Stoney Middleton
Well-dressing, late Jul.

Tideswell
Wakes Week, late Jun.
Well-dressing, late Jun/early Jul.
Male Voice Choir and Silver Band
Annual Concert, early Jul.

Winster
Pancake racing, Shrove Tuesday.
Winster Wakes Festivities,
late Jun–early Jul.

Wormhill
Well-dressing and demonstration,
late Aug.

Youlgreave
Well-dressing, late Jun.

TEA ROOMS

The Original Bakewell Pudding Shop
The Square, Bakewell,
Derbyshire, DE45 1BT
Tel: 01629 812193
www.bakewellpuddingshop.co.uk
Above the shop where Bakewell's
famed recipe was recreated, this
comfortable tea room has exposed
beams reminiscent of a medieval barn.
Indulge in sandwiches and pastries,
afternoon tea to a more filling meal,
but don't miss out on a generous
helping of Bakewell Pudding.

The Old Smithy Tea Rooms
Church Street, Monyash,
Derbyshire, DE45 1JH
Tel: 01629 810190
www.monyash.info
Set beside the village green and
ancient cross, the Old Smithy provides
supremely well for walkers and visitors
to this delightful old village. Although,
renowned for its all-day breakfast,
traditional cream teas and pastries are
its main draws.

Eyam Tea Rooms
The Square, Eyam,
Derbyshire, S32 5RB
Tel: 01433 631274
At the Town End part of Eyam and
overlooking the pretty square this tea
room has a particular reputation for
fine home-made cakes, gateaux and
scones. There's also a good choice of
vegetarian meals and snacks.

Monsal View Café
Monsal Head, Ashford in the Water,
Derbyshire, DE45 1NL
Tel: 01629 640346
Overlooking magnificent Monsal Dale
this friendly, stone-floored café with a
roaring fire in winter offers filling fare,
from snacks to restaurant meals and
Derbyshire cream teas.

HADDON HOUSE

MONSAL DALE

The Red Lion

Litton, near Tideswell,
Derbyshire, SK17 8QU
Tel: 01298 871458

Tiny beamed rooms, uneven stone floors and glowing logs in the hearths make this inn a magnet for pub aficionados. A friendly landlord, affable locals, great microbrewery beers and a very tasty menu make it one of the best in the Peak District.

The Lathkill Hotel

Over Haddon, Bakewell,
Derbyshire, DE45 1JE
Tel: 01629 812501

This long-established inn was built to serve lead-miners. Today's guests tuck into a mix of simple bar meals, inventive, top-notch dishes, and beers from Peak District breweries.

The Bull's Head Inn

Foolow, Derbyshire, S32 5QD
Tel: 01433 630873

A row of cottages in this peaceful hamlet forms this classic inn. The cosy interior features beams, flagstone floors, oak panelling, log fires and simple furnishings. To one end there is a smarter dining room; space here, then, for walkers, diners and locals to indulge in beers from the local Barn Brewery with the guarantee of good, filling fodder, including Sunday roasts.

The Barrel Inn

Bretton, Eyam, Derbyshire, S32 5QD
Tel: 01433 630856

Derbyshire's highest pub, The Barrel Inn stands right on the lip of Eyam Edge, giving immense views across the heart of the White Peak. Expect beers from Hardys and Hansons brewery and good size portions of tasty, but unpretentious pub food, served in cosy surroundings of antique seats, age-smoothed flagged floors, low beams, country prints and brass plates.

CURBAR EDGE

Derwent Valley
& Eastern Moors

BASLOW

CALVER & CURBAR

CHATSWORTH

CHESTERFIELD

CRICH

CROMFORD

DARLEY DALE

THE DERWENT DAMS

GRINDLEFORD

HATHERSAGE

MATLOCK

INTRODUCTION

A ribbon of high gritstone
moorland runs all the way
from Stocksbridge in the north
to Matlock in the south, which
serves as a buffer between
the industries and suburbs
of Sheffield and Chesterfield
and the main artery of the
Peaks, the River Derwent. At
the edge of the heather moors
are great shelves of gritstone,
etched by ancient ice into a
famous series of west-facing
cliffs or Edges. At the head of
the Derwent there are many
attractive villages, all quite
different, and several historic
houses, of which Chatsworth
House stands supreme.

HOT SPOTS

Unmissable attractions

Take a cable-car ride up the Heights of Abrahmam in Matlock Bath and admire the views down the length of the gorge...or experience whitewater rafting and kayaking in the narrow gorge, where there's plenty of turbulent water for both sports...explore the Derwent Dams on bike or foot...visit the pretty Peak villages of Frogatt, Curbar, Baslow and Stanage surrounded by mellow valley and skirted by woods and meadows...spend a day exploring the magnificent mansion and grounds of Chatsworth House...go in search of wildlife on the heather moorland above Beeley.

1

3 Crich Tram Museum
A fascinating place where visitors can ride on vintage trams, which run from a period street setting into attractive open countryside.

1 Curbar Edge
The little village of Curbar nestles in the Derwent Valley beneath rugged Curbar Edge, an area popular with both walkers and climbers.

2 Chatsworth House
Standing within superb parkland and gardens, Chatsworth House, often known as the 'Palace of the Peak', is a treasure trove of works of art.

BASLOW

The 18th-century turnpike road from Sheffield used to cross the River Derwent next to St Anne's Church in the oldest part of Baslow, called Bridge End. A modern bridge now spans the river a short distance to the south, making it possible to idle about the 17th-century triple-arched bridge and take a closer look at the little toll house (the doorway is just 3.5 feet/1m high) that guards it. Further along the lane on the west bank of the river stands Bubnell Hall, which is as old as the bridge, whilst on the east bank, above the main road, stands Baslow Hall, an early 20th-century copy that has been converted into the luxurious Fischer's Hotel.

On the far side of Baslow is Nether End, almost a village in itself, gathered around its own little Goose Green and with a row of pretty thatched cottages, which overlook Bar Brook. Thatched cottages are now quite rare in the area, although 'black thatch' (heather or turf) may once have been more widespread. Nether End marks the north entrance to the Chatsworth Estate and there is a touch of sophisticated comfort about everything; this applies equally to the nearby Cavendish Hotel, which contains some antiques from Chatsworth.

Further east along the Sheffield road the Bar Brook cuts a nick in the dramatic gritstone scarp, with Baslow Edge on one side and Birchen Edge on the other. A sea of bracken laps the footings of the rock faces, whilst the moorland above the Edge is a lonely wilderness of heather and the home of merlin and grouse. It was once the home of farmers too, in the Bronze Age, when the climate was a little kinder. It is astonishing to find field systems still visible from more than 3,000 years ago. Below Baslow Bar, just out of Nether End, it is also possible to see narrow fields separated by drystone walls that follow the old reverse-S pattern, the sign of ox-ploughing in medieval times.

CALVER & CURBAR

The Derwent divides these shrinking communities; Calver on the west bank lies in the lee of the limestone hills, whilst Curbar sits below a gritstone edge, close to the moors. A bridge built in the 18th-century links them, but this is bypassed by a crossing downstream and most people never notice Curbar as they swing west to Calver.

Calver has an industrial side to its character; shoes and sinks were among its products. The steel sink factory occupies what was once a cotton mill, built by Richard Arkwright in 1805 and employing up to 200 people. The mill's moment of glory came in the 1970s when its satanic profile won it the role of Colditz Castle in a television series.

Curbar is a quiet place on the shoulder of pastureland before Curbar Edge. The older features of the village include a circular pinfold or stock-pound, a covered well and circular trough, and a lock-up with a conical roof. These structures were fashioned in stone and built to last. In the 18th century nobody could foresee a time when sheep wouldn't stray, horses wouldn't be thirsty and men wouldn't get drunk.

The Chesterfield turnpike heads east out of Curbar, seeking the gap in the gritstone edge on the skyline. Great stone slabs were easily won from the Edge and were used for more than just millstones. On the tussocky pasture close to the village lies a small group of gravestones marking the final resting place of the Cundy family, who died of the plague in 1632 (more than 30 years before the Eyam outbreak). Further up, several slabs of rock bear biblical references, the work of a molecatcher-cum-preacher, Edwin Gregory, who worked on the Chatsworth Estate a century ago. Finally, as the road straightens and heads over the Bar Brook, there are drystone walls, guideposts and a clapper bridge, dating back to the packhorse era before the road became a turnpike in 1759.

CURBAR EDGE

Visit

CHATSWORTH DEER

The deer at Chatsworth are fallow deer, which were introduced into Britain by the Normans to grace their hunting forests. Fallow differ from the native red and roe deer in having a spotted coat and broad antlers. A visit to Chatsworth's glorious parkland can give the impression of an English version of the African Serengeti, with cattle, sheep and deer instead of wildebeest and impala.

CHATSWORTH

Towards the end of the 17th century, William Cavendish, the 4th Earl of Devonshire and soon to be made the 1st Duke for his part in putting William of Orange on the throne, decided his house needed a radical new look. For a while he tinkered with alterations, but finally knocked everything down and started again. Demolishing one great historic house to build another might seem an odd investment of a lifetime, but in those days great families were judged by their homes and gardens; fashion and taste was everything.

The Chatsworth House that rose from the rubble of the Elizabethan mansion was of a classical, Palladian style, to the duke's own design. It took about 30 years to complete and it set the seal on his new status – even some of the window frames were gilded on the outside. The irony is that he never saw it at its best. Great houses needed great gardens and grounds, and these took decades to establish. In the middle of the 18th century 'Capability' Brown and James Paine laid the foundations of what we see today by altering the course of the river and roads, building bridges and setting out woodland vistas.

The house is bursting with great works of art in the most superb settings; the Painted Hall is a work of art in itself, with huge, swirling scenes from the life of Julius Caesar by Louis Laguerre on the ceiling and upper part of the walls. Splendour

CHATSWORTH HOUSE

follows splendour as you progress through the house (a tour of about a third of a mile/0.5km), but one of the most engaging features that stays in the memory long after you have left the house is the wonderful trompe l'oeil painting of a violin on the inner door of the State Music Room.

None can deny the magnificence of the house itself, but the real secret of Chatsworth is its setting. From any direction it looks majestic, and from the southwest, approaching Edensor on a sunny evening, it can be breathtaking. On the horizon to the east are the high gritstone moors; in the middle distance are tiers of woodland, melting into ribbons and stands of beech and oak and rolling parkland; and in the foreground winds the River Derwent. The front of the house reflects the peach-glow of evening sunlight to perfection; around it are superb formal gardens and the fine Emperor fountain. This is a view the 1st Duke could only have dreamed about.

Insight

BILBERRY TIME

Purple bird droppings on moorland walls are a sign that it is bilberry time. Bilberry (blaeberry in Scotland and blueberry in America) grows on the slopes and along the road verges of Beeley Moor. The bell-shaped flowers give way to glorious dark purple berries in July; despite being rather inconspicuous, the fruit bushes are quickly stripped by grouse, foxes and other wild animals. But just 30 minutes of gathering should produce enough fruit for a small pie. The taste is delicious.

The Chatsworth Estate stretches far and wide and includes grouse moors, working farmland and estate villages. Of the villages Edensor catches the eye first. Until the 1830s the village stood a little closer to the river but the 6th Duke had it moved further back, out of sight. The new houses were a hotchpotch of styles; Italian, Swiss, almost anything but vernacular English. Only one house

Activity

WILDLIFE OF THE MOORLAND

Of all the heather moorland in the Peaks the expanse above Beeley is probably the best for wildlife. This has been due in part to its isolation and lack of access, but now it is possible to explore several of its finest areas without damaging the most sensitive ecological sites. You don't have to walk very far to find wildlife as the roadside walls are one of the best places to look. Lichen-coloured moths, such as the grey chi and glaucous shears sit on the stone walls, while the full-grown caterpillars of emperor and northern eggar moths like to sun themselves on the tops of bilberry bushes and heather clumps.

with the Chatsworth Farm Shop selling excellent local produce, a pub and a microbrewery.

Just outside the Chatsworth Estate to the south, but within its influence and historic ownership, lies Beeley. This old working village, tucked neatly away and with many of the elements of a much older settlement, has quite a refreshing character. A tannery once stood beside the brook, and there was an estate-built school and a barn to house the coal wagons that supplied the Chatsworth estate glasshouses with fuel. Over the years most of the old buildings have been put to other uses, but fortunately not the public house (The Devonshire Arms), which is still a good excuse for stopping on the way up to the moors.

CHESTERFIELD

The tall spire of St Mary's and All Saints church would have tapered to an elegant pencil-point if its timbers had been properly seasoned. Instead it stands crooked and

of the original village remains, called Park Cottage, but known at one time as Naboth's Vineyard. The biblical reference relates to the owner in 1838, who is supposed to have refused to sell or be relocated. Just 1 mile (1.6km) to the northwest lies Pilsley, more compact than Edensor,

CHESTERFIELD

A.D. 1688.
IN A ROOM WHICH FORMERLY
EXISTED AT THE END OF THIS
COTTAGE (WHAT IS LEFT OF THE
OLD COCK & PYNOT) THE EARL
OF DANBY THE EARL OF DEVONSHIRE
AND MR JOHN D'ARCY ELDEST SON
OF THE EARL OF HOLDERNESS MET
SOMETIME IN 1688 TO CONCERT
MEASURES WHICH RESULTED IN THE
REVOLUTION OF THAT YEAR

twisted, a unique landmark, famous for the wrong reasons. Medieval Chesterfield was a prosperous town of guilds; it aspired to have a church that was worthy of its status and was full of fine buildings. Many of these still exist behind shop-fronts and occasionally appear when renovation takes place.

Chesterfield is an industrial town. Its heart still beats in time with the coalfields and it is worth visiting for its old inns and good humour. It lies outside the Peak District, but serves its eastern flanks and is a gateway from the M1.

To the north of Chesterfield lies the village of Old Whittington, where a group of daring conspirators led by the Earl of Devonshire met in 1688 to hatch a plot to overthrow the Catholic King James II. The plot was successful; the country welcomed William of Orange and the course of history was changed. The meeting took place in a little thatched inn called the Cock and Pynot, now known as Revolution House and a modest tourist attraction, furnished in 17th-century style and with a film telling the story of the Revolution. Just 2 miles (3.2km) away is Newbold Moor, where the tiny Norman Chapel was attacked in the same year by a mob of Protestants. The chapel, now restored, has a simple weather-beaten charm. Nearby is Tapton House, the home in later life of George Stephenson, the pioneer railway engineer.

CRICH

Perched atop a limestone anticline, the monument on Crich Stand glows from a distance looking like a lighthouse set on alabaster cliffs above a shadowy sea. Three beacon-towers have stood here, but each time they were destroyed by lightning strikes. The present structure dates from 1921 and is a memorial to the men of the Sherwood Foresters Regiment killed in the service of the Crown. The 63-foot (19m) tower offers views across eight counties.

Below the Stand lies a busy working quarry, still eating away at the hill. In its early years George Stephenson built a narrow-gauge railway so that the limestone could be carried to kilns at Ambergate. Now, the worked-out shelf of the quarry is the location of Crich Tramway Village, where more than 40 trams from all over the world are housed. Many are in working order and run every few minutes through a period street, then into open countryside. Along the street is the Georgian façade of the Derby Assembly Rooms, relocated here in 1972 after the original building in Derby's Market Place had been badly damaged by fire. Other attractions include an exhibition hall and a high-tech sound and vision experience.

Crich is a quiet place; many of the houses are 18th or early 19th century and were once the homes of stockingers, working on knitting frames by the light of top-storey windows. The Jovial Dutchman pub dates from about the same time.

CROMFORD

Road, rail, river and canal run side by side south from Cromford. At first sight it is hard to understand why transport was so important to the place – until 1771 it had been little more than a just a cluster of small cottages around an old packhorse bridge. Until the industrialist Richard Arkwright arrived and set to work to build a cotton mill. Power was plentiful, in the shape of Bonsall Brook and Cromford Moor Sough (the drainage waterway from nearby lead workings) and there was a ready supply of cheap labour due to the decline of the lead-mining industry. Within just a few years Arkwright was rich and the village was a cradle of the Industrial Revolution; three mills were built and lines of gritstone terraced houses accommodated a workforce who laboured, for very long hours, in factories rather than in their own homes. For good and ill the 'Satanic Mills' were the birthplace of the urban working class.

Visit

A CANAL NATURE RESERVE

Downstream of the Leawood viaduct the Derwent Valley is particularly beautiful; in spring wild daffodils grow on the riverside pastures and the oak woodlands ring with the sounds of wood warblers, redstarts and pied flycatchers. Located just below Whatstandwell, the overgrown canal is a nature reserve, a haven busy with wildlife; frogs and grass snakes, dragonflies and kingfishers. Take the train to Ambergate and it's possible to walk along the towpath to the next station at Whatstandwell, where there is also an excellent pub.

Cromford Canal was built in the early 1790s to link up with the Erewash Canal, which then ran southeast to Nottingham. Cromford Wharf marked its northern terminus, at the mill. A turnpike road was opened up in 1817, then in the 1830s the Cromford and High Peak Railway was constructed, which linked the Cromford Canal with the Peak Forest Canal at Whaley Bridge, thus linking the Trent with the Mersey. In its early years this busy 33-mile (53km) wagonway employed horses on the level stretches and steam winding engines on the inclines. It was considered an extension of the canals and the stations were called wharfs, but by the middle of the 19th century the age of steam had arrived and the Midland Railway was extended north from Ambergate to meet the High Peak line.

Arkwright's Cromford Mill is now undergoing a restoration programme by the Arkwright Society, who aim to create a lasting monument to his extraordinary genius. There are guided tours, and a visitor centre on the site interprets the mill's heyday. Cromford Canal is popular for family picnics, and there is a towpath walk to High Peak Junction, where there is another visitor centre. The Cromford and High Peak Railway closed in 1967 and is now a popular recreational trail, the High Peak Trail (new Pennine Bridleway follows it).

Cromford is made prettier by its large pond, behind the market square, and the Greyhound Hotel (built by Arkwright in 1778). The pond was originally one of the impounding reservoirs to hold water from the Bonsall Brook, but its margins are now the home of ducks and swans. On the other side of the A6, close to the wharf and within sight of Arkwright's elegant homes of Rock House and Willesley Castle, lies the old bridge and its ruined chapel, at the site of the 'crooked ford' that became Cromford.

DARLEY DALE

Four settlements along the Derwent were bound together under the name Darley Dale a century ago, but the ties were never strong enough to give the place an identity. The A6 has now replaced the railway as the nub of the community, leaving Darley with an artery but no heart.

Darley was the home of Sir Joseph Whitworth, the man who invented the screw thread. Munitions, which included a rifle that fired hexagonal bullets, nuts and bolts, and machine tools soon made him rich, and he bestowed much of his wealth on the local community by not only building a Whitworth Hospital but a Whitworth Hotel, a Whitworth Park and an Institute. Victorian benefactors liked to have their good deeds recognised, but in Whitworth's case his generosity won him few friends and he was not popular. He lived at Stancliffe Hall (not open), guarding his privacy behind high walls and hedges, and when he died in 1887 his dreams of a model village died too.

Beside the A6 lies Stancliffe Quarry. Stone from here was sent to London, where it was used to pave Trafalgar Square and the Embankment. Below this, on the other side of the railway line and on a low mound above the river flats, is Churchtown. Here stands the fine parish church of St Helens, founded by the Normans but rebuilt at the same time as the Old Hall

LADYBOWER RESERVOIR

in the 14th century, which once stood a little way further to the north. Most of what is visible on the outside is the result of 19th-century restoration, but there are still plenty of interesting things to see inside; Saxon stones, painted wall designs, the tomb of Sir John de Darley (heart in hands), and the private pew of the reclusive, Sir Joseph Whitworth. The south transept has a stained-glass window by William Morris and Co, produced in the 1860s. The scenes depicted are from the *Song of Solomon*, the chunky figures were by Burne-Jones and the angels probably by William Morris. Victorian stained glass doesn't get any better. (Please note that the church is locked when not in use, but the key-holder's telephone number is posted in the porch.)

Above Darley and Northwood lie open fields and woodland before the Derwent meets the Wye at Rowsley. These days the village of Rowsley is most notable as a gateway to the Peak District on the A6, but it used to serve as a railway village with marshalling yards and a large dairy (to supply London with dairy products via the milk train). The railway closed in the late 1960s and the Station Hotel is now the Grouse and Claret pub. Nearby are the fine Peacock Hotel, a 17th-century manor house, and Caudwell's Mill, an old turbine-driven corn mill. The 19th-century mill is now a an interesting craft centre but it still produces flour and visitors can stroll along the paths beside the mill race and alongside the Wye.

THE DERWENT DAMS

Engineers had their eye on Derwent Dale for decades before work began at Howden Reservoir in 1901. It was the perfect spot; a long deep groove through solid millstone grit, bleak rain-washed moors all around, and only a scattered farming community to relocate. After Howden came Derwent Reservoir, which was completed in 1916. Ladybower, the last and largest, was inaugurated

Activity

'TIN TOWN'

Car parks and cycle hire make it easy to explore the western side of the Derwent Valley, along the shores of all three reservoirs and through the forest. By Derwent Reservoir and just south of Birchinlee the road passes beside the site of 'Tin Town', which was once a settlement of corrugated-iron houses provided for the navvies who built the upper reservoirs. For a decade at the beginning of the 20th century it was a self-contained community a thousand strong, with its own school and railway station; all that remains are a few grass-decked foundations and terraces.

to Sheffield, and the rest is shared between Derby and Nottingham.

Although the sheer scale of the engineering works is impressive, it is the creation of a Canadian-style landscape that draws visitors – big views over great sheets of water, curtains of mist and conifers decked in snow; definitely not very British, but a grand prospect. The forest looks dark and dreary, and there is no doubt that alien conifers are not a substitute for native oak when it comes to bio-diversity. Even so, there are a few surprises. Red squirrels keep a toe-hold here, and in good seed years the local chaffinches are joined by flocks of crossbills. Goshawks are widespread but furtive, except in the early spring when they soar high in display flight over the wooded cloughs.

The Derwent Dams are famous for their drowned villages; when there is a drought thousands of people flock to see a few uncovered stones. The only building to cheat the flood was the Derwent

in 1945; as well as flooding 2 miles (3.2km) of the Derwent Valley this also spread up the Woodlands Valley, but not very far because there would be the risk of landslips. Ladybower now holds about 6,000 million gallons of water, the others slightly less; more than a third of the water is piped to Leicester, another third

packhorse bridge, dismantled and rebuilt further up the valley to span the river at Slippery. The legendary 617 Dambusters Squadron practised at Derwent Dams before their famous raid on The Ruhr in 1943.

GRINDLEFORD

The best way to arrive at Grindleford is by train, either from the east, through the 3.5-mile (5.6km) Totley Tunnel (the second longest tunnel in the country) or from the west, back-tracking down the line from Hathersage along one of the prettiest silvan stretches of the Derwent. Before the advent of the Hope Valley line Grindleford was little more than a turnpike crossing (the toll house still stands, next to the bridge), and the nearby settlements of Upper and Nether Padley were small enough to be lost among the trees. However, the villages bloomed with the opening of the railway station in 1898; most of the houses jostling the slopes and terraces were built by the resulting wave of Sheffield commuters, but not so many that the villages merged or lost their woodland backdrop.

Grindleford Station is actually in Upper Padley. A few hundred yards towards the Derwent, over Burbage Brook and past the converted watermill, lie the ruins of Padley Hall. Very little remains of the 14th-century mansion except foundations. It was once the proud home of the Fitzherbert family, who were Roman Catholics and had the misfortune to be caught harbouring priests at a time when it was illegal to celebrate Mass. In fact the timing could not have been worse; the Spanish Armada had set sail and the country was on the lookout for spies. The two priests, Nicholas Garlick and Robert Ludlam (local men who had been trained in France), were taken to Derby where they were hung, drawn and quartered. John Fitzherbert died in the Tower 30 years later. Padley Hall became the home of one of Elizabeth I's chief priest-catchers before becoming a farm.

The gatehouse, which had survived as a barn, was restored in 1933 and is now a chapel; a pilgrimage in memory of the martyrs takes place each July.

In the other direction, following the Burbage Brook upstream, runs a lovely network of paths through Padley Gorge. The boulder-strewn slopes of the gorge are covered in a thick layer of mosses and ferns, thriving in the damp shadows of the ancient oak wood. The trees are sessile oaks rather than pedunculate oaks; the obvious difference is that the sessile acorns are 'sessile' and don't have stalks. Acorns are an autumn bonanza for birds and animals; badgers and squirrels, jays and woodpigeons all make the most of the easy pickings. The spring bonanza is the plentiful crop of caterpillars, gathered from the leaves by migrants, such as pied flycatchers and wood warblers.

Padley Gorge is part of the National Trust's delightful Longshaw Estate. Longshaw Lodge, built as

Insight

HAUNTING REMAINS

Before World War II, Ashopton and Derwent, were small villages of stone-built cottages, but the building of the Ladybower Reservoir shattered the lives of the locals. After the completion of its dam in 1943 the reservoir gradually filled up, and by 1946 was above the tops of the rooftops. The old gateposts of Derwent Hall still survive by the roadside and a noticeboard shows the positions of some of the original buildings in Derwent village, but after a dry spell the water level can sometimes fall sufficiently for you to see the crumbling walls and foundations of the village, surrounded by crazed drying mud.

a shooting lodge for the Dukes of Rutland, stands beside the B6521 in attractive grounds. These are now the core of a country park, from where there is access to the wild moorland above Froggatt Edge. The views all along this most famous Edge are superb, westward over

LADYBOWER RESERVOIR

HERE LIES BURIED

LITTLE JOHN
THE FRIEND & LIEUTENANT OF
ROBIN HOOD
HE DIED IN A COTTAGE (NOW DESTROYED)
TO THE EAST OF THE CHURCHYARD
THE GRAVE IS MARKED BY
THIS OLD HEADSTONE & FOOTSTONE
AND IS UNDERNEATH THIS OLD YEW TREE

the White Peak and the Dark. To the east rises White Edge on Big Moor, running south to Swine Sty, a fascinating Bronze Age settlement in a 'fossilised' landscape of prehistoric fields, picked out among beds of bracken and heather.

HATHERSAGE

Stanage Edge divides featureless moorland from the verdant Derwent. Prehistoric pathways, Roman roads and packhorse trails criss-cross the wild moors and converge below the confluence of the Derwent and the Noe rivers. On the raised south-facing shoulder of the valley lies Hathersage ('Heather's Edge'), a village built on passing trade and farming. Millstones were a speciality in the 18th century, hewn directly from quarry faces. Then came the Industrial Revolution and five mills were built, to make pins and needles. The mills had a short life, as did the men who ground the needle-points and had to breathe in the lethal dust.

Whether there ever was a real Little John, or John Nailor, hardly matters. Most visitors want to believe that it really is his grave they see in Hathersage's churchyard. The grave close to the south porch has been excavated several times without producing any bones, though there is a story that a huge thighbone was unearthed here in 1784. In fact the half-hidden stones at the head and foot of the grave were probably set there as the village perch: the standard measure used to mark out acres of land in the days of open-field or strip farming.

The most interesting buildings in Hathersage are along the main road and off School Lane. Past 15th-century Hathersage Hall and Farm, and up the narrow Church Bank, it is possible to walk around Bank Top, a green knoll overlooking the alder-lined Hood Brook and valley. The church crouches on the grassy brow. To the south stands Bell House and The Bell Room, once an inn and barn beside the village green and stocks;

197

TEA ROOMS

The Grindleford Spring Water Company

Station Approach, Grindleford, Derbyshire, S32 2JA
Tel: 01433 631011

Known to generations of walkers and cyclists, this venerable café is tucked next to the west portal of Totley Tunnel, on the Sheffield to Manchester line. Enjoy the full breakfasts, snacks and pint mugs of tea or coffee on offer here.

Post Office Tea Room

Edensor, Derbyshire, DE45 1PH
Tel: 01246 582283

This charming tea room is tucked away just behind the village church and is an integral part of the post-office stores, hidden amidst the peaceful byroads of the estate village. Expect quality cream teas and dainties, tasty snacks and soups, many made using Chatsworth Estate produce.

The Country Parlour

Caudwell's Mill, Rowsley, Derbyshire, DE4 2EB
Tel: 01629 733185

The tea rooms, squeezed between the River Derwent and the mill race, serve scones, cakes and pastries baked on site, many using flour milled next door. Rest easy in old chapel seats and pews, before visiting the craft centre and the mill.

Bookshop Café

Scarthin Books, The Promenade, Cromford, Derbyshire, DE4 3QF
Tel: 01629 823272
www.scarthinbooks.com

Books, as well as on-site arts and crafts exhibitions, draw the eye at this quirky little vegetarian café in Cromford. Home-bakes and teabread, pizzas, Fairtrade coffee, nine kinds of tea and thick soups made from home-grown vegetables are on offer.

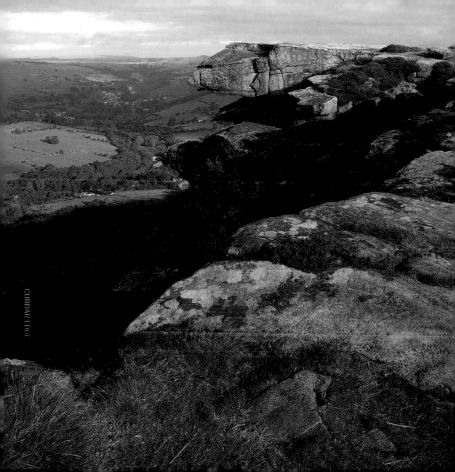

CURBAR EDGE

Dark Peak

CASTLETON

EDALE

GLOSSOP

HAYFIELD

HOLMFIRTH

HOPE

LANGSETT

LONGDENDALE

SADDLEWORTH

THE SNAKE PASS

HOT SPOTS

Unmissable attractions

Stay at Castleton, which suffers from a surfeit of tourists, but is a good base for exploring the area...walk part, or all, of the Pennine Way, Britain's first and toughest long-distance footpath, which has its southern terminus at Edale...strap on your hiking books and follow in the footsteps of the revolutionary Trespass at Kinder Scout, the Peaks highest hill...go walking in Snake Pass and enjoy the truly wild isolation of the moors...go in search of industrial heritage at Glossop or Hope...discover the impressively sited ruins of Peveril Castle...go deep beneath the castle and explore Speedwell Cavern, an old lead mine that descends 2000 feet (600m) or visit some of Britain's deepest and most challenging caves.

1

1 Kinder Scout
Celebrating the climb to the top of Kinder Scout, and enjoying the reward of far-reaching views, which take in the Kinder Reservoir in the distance.

2 The Pennine Way
Edale marks the start of the Pennine Way, which runs for 256 miles (412km) to Kirk Yetholm, just over the border in Scotlands.

3 Edale
A cyclist tackles the winding Edale road in the Dark Peak. Less arduous routes for cyclists, and walkers, include the Sett Valley Trail which runs from New Mills to Hayfield.

4 Peak Cavern, Castleton
The cave extends deep into the hillside so, when visiting, remember to wear warm clothes, even on a summer's day, as it will be much colder underground.

3

CASTLETON

Castles and caves cast a potent spell; Castleton sometimes suffers from a surfeit of tourists, but there is so much of interest along the upper reach of the Hope Valley that it is impossible not to be drawn into the busy little village, at least as a base from which to wander.

The curtain of high hills at the head of the valley rises to an impressive 1,695 feet (517m) at Mam Tor, less than 2 miles (3.2km) to the northwest of the village. Bands of shale and gritstone give the breast-shaped dome of this 'mother-mountain' a terraced appearance; more though importantly, the shale is unstable and the whole hillside is gradually slumping down into the valley, taking the old main road with it. In recent years the fate of the road has drawn as many sightseers as the more conventional tourist attractions in the area.

The tumbled stonework of an Iron Age hill fort rings the top of Mam Tor; hill forts were a sign of

Visit

OAK APPLE DAY

Oak Apple Day, 29 May, is celebrated in Castleton by a glorious pub crawl, involving a procession led by the 'King' and 'Queen', both in Restoration costume and on horseback; the King is completely covered in a great cone of flowers. A silver band plays the traditional tune *Pudding in a Lantern*, girls dance and everyone welcomes the summer. This is Garland day; obscure, colourful and intoxicating. The words of a song capture the spirit of the event:

Thou doesno' know, and I dono' know
What they han i' Brada;
An owd cow's head, and a piece o' bread,
And a pudding baked in a lantern

prestige and status among hostile tribes in those faraway times, and this site must have been the power-base of an important chieftain. When the Romans arrived the local community had to learn a new way

HOLLINS CROSS

Visit

'WHETHER THE WEATHER BE WET'

Edale is not a place to linger in the rain; 60 inches (152cm) a year fall on Kinder, and the Booths get their share. Nor is there very much cover. On crisp winter mornings it can be cold in the valley, as frost rolls down from the summits, but this is certainly the time to appreciate the elemental landscape and the far horizons.

and Kinder Downfall, the waterfall that sometimes gets blown uphill in the teeth of the western gales. A stiff walk, but worthwhile for the views to the west are very special.

GLOSSOP

Textiles breathed life into Glossop; there was water power and coal aplenty and a keen and hardworking workforce who came from Stockport and Manchester. At the turn of the 19th century there were more than 56 mills in the eight townships of Glossopdale; most were large cotton mills, but there were also paper mills, ropewalks and woollen mills. Not many thrived; those that did were obliged to modernise with the times and took to power looms, which were steam-driven and needed more water and more coal.

The settlement expanded in the early 19th century under the patronage of the Duke of Norfolk and at one time it was named Howard Town (Howard is the family name of the duke), to distinguish it from Old Glossop, the village uphill to the east. The name Glossop came from Glott Hop, 'hop' being a valley and 'glott' a much earlier lord of the manor. But it was the Howards who left the greatest mark on the new community and who were responsible for most of the town's important buildings, such as the Market Hall and the Railway Station. The heart of Glossop is Norfolk Square, which still has a prim elegance and is surrounded by interesting shops, including a small heritage centre.

23

PD&NCFPS
1906

FOOTPATH
TO BIRCH VALE VIA
RIDGE TOP & BRIDLE
Rᴰ TO NEW MILLS &ᴄ
OVER THE HILL TOP
ALTITUDE 1085 FEET

EDALE

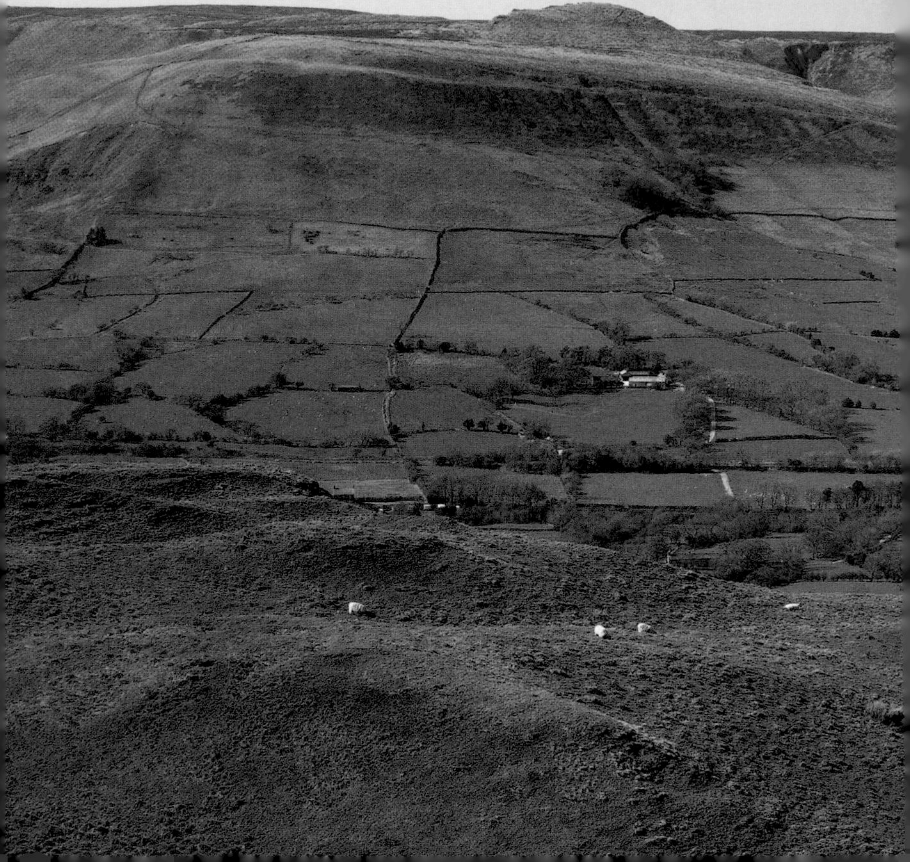

Glossop suffered disastrously when the cotton industry collapsed in the 1920s, and it took decades to recover. Overspill housing from the 1960s has affected the character of the town too, but there are some fascinating nooks and crannies, hidden away. Just beyond the housing estate of Gamesley lies the remains of the Agricolan Roman fort of Melandra Castle, whilst to the north of the town, near Howard Park, is Mouselow or Castle Hill, with important Bronze Age and Iron Age associations and the site of a motte and bailey built by William de Peverel. Glossop's roads to the east lead to Longdendale and the Snake Pass, whilst only a few miles to the west is the M67 and Manchester.

HAYFIELD

The picturesque name and rural setting disguise Hayfield's industrial past; the village once hummed and rattled to the sound of cotton and paper mills, calico printing and dye works. It has also resounded to marching feet and cries of protest – in 1830 a mob of 1,000 mill workers gathered to demand a living wage and were dispersed by hussars. Eleven men appeared at Derby Assizes as a result, but the cotton industry was in terminal decline and all the anger was in vain. A century later, on 24 April 1932, Hayfield was the starting point for the 'mass trespass' of ramblers onto Kinder Scout. This protest eventually resulted in 'the right to roam'.

Hayfield is a peaceful little village, catering for tourists of all kinds. It has plenty of little cafés and restaurants with quaint and inventive names. One of the most revealing places to while away a few minutes is by the bridge, next to the courtyard of the Royal Hotel, which looks out over the River Sett, from the war memorial to the jumble of cottages and sloping roofs at the back of Church Street. Nearby is St Matthew's Church, built on the foundations of an older church washed away in a flood.

Serious walkers head east out of the village, up and over the green foothills to the russet expanse of the Kinder plateau. Families and explore other easy-going ramblers head west along the Sett Valley Trail towards New Mills. The car park at the start of this 3-mile (4.8km) trail, separated from the main village by the A624, was once the railway station, and the trail follows the course of the single-track line.

In 2007, the 75th anniversary of the Mass Trespass was marked by the opening of the Trespass Trail, a 14-mile (22.6km) walk following the route of the original trespassers.

HOLMFIRTH

Before the BBC television series *Last of the Summer Wine* became a national institution, the most famous comic characters to come out of Holmfirth were depicted on postcards published by Bamforths. Saucy seaside cartoons became a serious business for the family firm just after the Great War; they had already pioneered lantern slides and the motion picture industry but were outflanked in the end by Hollywood.

The town of Holmfirth is a gem, built at the confluence of the Holme and the Ribble, where the Norman Earl Warren built a corn mill. For several centuries the lower valley was left to the wild wood and the hilltop towns of Cartworth, Upperthong and Wooldale prospered, combining farming with weaving. There are fine stone farmhouses and cottages on the upper slopes of the valley, often absorbed into the outskirts of the newer town, to tell the tale of prosperity. With the expansion of the cotton mills in the mid 19th-century tiers of three-storey terraced cottages sprang up lower and lower into the valley and eventually cotton mills crowded the riverside. The fast-flowing river was harnessed but never tamed; it still floods when the Pennine snows melt too quickly.

Holmfirth has to be explored at a gentle pace, because most of

valley was dammed to create five reservoirs, and this has so altered the character of the place that it sometimes looks like an oasis in a desert; green woodland and pasture encircles pools of silver, over which white sailing dinghies scud.

Longdendale is a favourite place for day trips out of Manchester, and the cultural roots of Tintwistle are entwined with the old Lancashire cotton mills. The waters of the Etherow were harnessed to power the mills and were dammed to provide water for the city. Railway lines were laid to link Manchester and Sheffield, following the valley up to Woodhead and the Prough, a 3-mile (4.8km) tunnel below the moors. But now all that is in the distant past; the weavers' cottages of Tintwistle are now picturesque and the course of the railway is a footpath. Nevertheless, the dale still serves the city in its own way and remains part of its heritage.

The graveyard of Woodhead Chapel, set on a shoulder above the banks of the upper reservoir, contains the last resting place of navvies and their families who died of cholera while the second railway tunnel was being built in 1849.

Crowden, above Torside Reservoir, is a famous youth hostel on the Pennine Way and is a welcome sight to walkers after the rigours of Bleaklow to the south or Black Hill to the north. Apart from a few isolated farms and an Information Centre there are no other settlements in the valley; despite the scenery Longdendale often suffers from a wild climate.

SADDLEWORTH

The gorge of the river Tame forms the boundary of the National Park in the northwest. Slicing between Saddleworth Moor and the West Pennines, this defile hosts a string of picturesque gritstone villages that breathe Yorkshire charm and character into an area with a history stretching back to the Romans (the site of a fortlet stands beside the remote reservoirs at Castleshaw). Saddleworth itself is a nebulous area; there's no village of that name here – the great sweep of moors arcing west from Holmfirth and the villages take that collective name, an area that was part of Yorkshire's West Riding until 1974 and decidedly proud of this fact. The largest village is Uppermill, strung alongside the Huddersfield Narrow Canal and crammed with craft and antique shops, restaurants and inns; the Saddleworth Museum offers a succinct overview of the area. Just to the north, locks rise to Britain's longest canal tunnel at Standedge, over 3 miles (5km) long.

The most charismatic village is Dobcross, huddled around a tiny cobbled square stapled to the end of Harrop Edge, from which narrow lanes and ginnels lined with three-storey weaver's cottages plummet to old mills in the valley bottom. Film buffs may recognise the square from the film *Yanks*. Further up the Tame, Delph retains perhaps the most

WHAT IS A NATIONAL PARK?

Britain's National Parks are not national property. Most of the land is still privately owned, but the area is administered by a National Park Authority. It is their task to strike an appropriate – and often fragile – balance between the conservation of the park's landscape, architecture and wildlife, while still ensuring that the local people and landowners can make a living and that the millions of visitors and walkers have access to use and appreciate the park's landscape. The National Park Authority in the Peak District operates a number of Information Centres, such as the one at Langsett, which provides a wide range of information, publications and organises walks and talks in and about the area.

'industrial' feel of all the villages, its mills gradually morphing into trendy apartments below bluffs and crags.

Linking these and the other villages of Saddleworth is the Longwood Thump Rushcart Festival.

Visit

THE SNAKE PASS INN

The Snake Pass Inn was built in 1821 as Lady Clough House, when the original medieval track was transformed into a turnpike road. If any visitor should need a reminder about how remote this hostelry is, there is a milestone outside the inn that records the 21 miles to Manchester and 17 miles to Sheffield. The low stone-built inn is an ideal place to stop for refreshment. Food is served most days of the week and a range of accommodation is available.

Held over the second weekend after the 12th August, this celebration centres on a cart, pulled by teams of men, that is decorated by a high pyramid of rushes, atop which a hapless soul must sit in a chair whilst touring the churches and inns of the area. The phrase 'Going on the Wagon' is said to originate here.

A visit to the Church Inn, high above Uppermill, where the festival is based, will reveal much.

In the graveyard next door is a fascinating memorial to victims of a double murder – the "Bill o' Jacks murders", unsolved since 1832. Myriad footpaths string southwards to some fine, challenging walks around and above Dovestone Reservoir, set in a landscape of cloughs, moors, edges and wind-sculpted pinnacles.

THE SNAKE PASS

Weather warnings on television and radio have made The Snake Pass famous; when the sun is shining across the rest of the Pennines, The Snake Pass, the A57 between Sheffield and Manchester, may be closed because of severe blizzards.

The road from Ladybower and the Woodlands Valley strikes northwest, sheltered on a shoulder of the River Ashop, but after Lady Clough it has nowhere to hide and crosses a windswept desert at 1,680 feet (512m). Bleaklow lies to the north, Kinder Scout to the south. In places the peat has been stripped

ACKNOWLEDGEMENTS

The Automobile Association would like to thank the following photographers, companies and picture libraries for their assistance in the preparation of this book.

Abbreviations for the picture credits are as follows – (t) top; (b) bottom; (c) centre; (l) left; (r) right; (AA) AA World Travel Library.

2/3 AA/M Birkitt; 5 AA/T Mackie; 6 AA/T Mackie; 9 AA/T Mackie; 12/3 AA/T Mackie; 14 AA/T Mackie; 15 AA/T Mackie; 16 AA/T Mackie; 17t AA/M Birkitt; 17b AA/T Mackie; 19 AA/T Mackie; 20 AA/T Mackie; 23 AA/T Mackie; 24 AA/T Mackie; 26 AA/T Mackie; 28/9 AA/A Midgley; 30 AA/T Mackie; 31l AA/T Mackie; 31r AA/T Mackie; 32 AA/T Mackie; 35 AA/T Mackie; 38/9 AA/T Mackie; 41 AA/T Mackie; 42 AA/V Greaves; 46/7 AA/T Mackie; 49 AA/T Mackie; 50/1 AA/T Mackie; 59 AA/A Tryner; 60 AA/T Mackie; 62 AA/M Birkitt; 64/5 AA/A J Hopkins; 66 AA/T Mackie; 67t AA/T Mackie; 67b AA/T Mackie; 69 AA/T Mackie; 70/1 AA/P Baker; 73 AA/T Mackie; 74/5 AA/T Mackie; 76 AA/A J Hopkins; 79 AA/T Mackie; 80 AA/T Mackie; 82/3 AA/T Mackie; 84 AA/A J Hopkins; 87 AA/J Mottershaw; 88 AA/A J Hopkins; 90/1 AA/A J Hopkins; 93 AA/T Mackie; 94 AA/T Mackie; 97 AA/T Mackie; 98/9 AA/T Mackie; 100 AA/A J Hopkins; 107 AA/T Mackie; 108 AA/M Birkitt; 110 AA/T Mackie; 112/3 AA/T Mackie; 114 AA/T Mackie; 115t AA/T Mackie; 115b AA/M Birkitt; 116 AA/T Mackie; 119 AA/T Mackie; 120 AA/T Mackie; 123 AA/T Mackie; 126/7 AA/P Baker; 128 AA/A J Hopkins; 130/1 AA/T Mackie; 133 AA/T Mackie; 134 AA/T Mackie; 137 AA/A J Hopkins; 138/9 AA/T Mackie; 140 AA/T Mackie; 143 AA/T Mackie; 146/7 AA/T Mackie; 155 AA/P Baker; 156 AA/T Mackie; 158 AA/T Mackie; 160/1 AA/T Mackie; 162 AA/T Mackie; 163t AA/A Midgley; 163b AA/T Mackie; 166/7 AA/T Mackie; 169 AA/A Midgley; 170/1 AA/J Beazley; 172 AA/A Midgley; 175 AA/A J Hopkins; 176 AA/T Mackie; 178/9 AA/T Mackie; 181 AA/T Mackie; 182/3 AA/T Mackie; 186/7 AA/T Mackie; 188 AA/T Mackie; 191 AA/T Mackie; 194/5 AA/M Birkitt; 196 AA/A J Hopkins; 198/9 AA/T Mackie; 201 AA/T Mackie; 207 AA/T Mackie; 208 AA/T Mackie; 210 AA/T Mackie; 212/3 AA/T Mackie; 214 AA/T Mackie; 215 AA/M Birkitt; 216 The AA; 217 AA/T Mackie; 218 AA/T Mackie; 222/3 AA/T Mackie; 225 AA/A Midgley; 226/7 AA/T Mackie; 231 AA/T Mackie; 232 AA/T Mackie; 235 AA/A J Hopkins; 239 AA/T Mackie; 240 AA/A J Hopkins; 247 AA/T Mackie; 248 AA/T Mackie.

Every effort has been made to trace the copyright holders, and we apologise in advance for any accidental errors. We would be happy to apply the corrections in the following edition of this publication.

away to reveal a surface of shattered stones, which is how the glaciers left the place after the Ice Age. There are no trees, no barns or walls. Not a good place to be stuck in a car.

Of course, the remote wildness of The Snake is irresistible and in fine weather, it can be magical. The upper Woodlands Valley is dotted with old farms and birch-lined cloughs. Most of the Peak District has been designated as an Environmentally Sensitive Area, which means that farmers get special payments for managing the land with conservation as a priority. In the case of the high moors, the most important thing is the stocking rate – fewer sheep are now overwintered on the heather, and this benefits the flora and fauna.

A tributary of the Ashop runs north to Alport Dale and Alport Castle, which is not a castle at all, but an outcrop of rock; this is accessible by a bridleway and makes a good walk. The barn of Alport Castle Farm is used on the first Sunday in July each year for a Lovefeast service. These 'love feasts' originated during the 18th-century religious revival that was spearheaded by the Wesley brothers. They converted multitudes of workers, from mines and mills, farms and factories, to a pattern of religious life which inspired them to build a number of 'wayside Bethels' in remote places. Along with field preaching, their ministers organised camp meetings and covenant services, incorporating 'love feasts', which were based on the meetings of the early Church.

Back on the Snake Road there are two or three farms and cottages before you reach the lonely Snake Pass Inn. At the top of Lady Clough, on the highest and most featureless ground, The Snake Pass is crossed by the Pennine Way, close to a paved trackway named Doctor's Gate, after a doctor from Longdendale who, legend has it, challenged the devil to a horse race and won. It's enough to send a chill down your spine.

DARK PEAK

TOURIST INFORMATION CENTRES

Glossop
The Heritage Centre, Henry Street.
Tel: 01457 855920

Holmfirth
49–51 Huddersfield Road.
Tel: 01484 222444

Saddleworth
High Street, Uppermill, Oldham.
Tel: 01457 870336

NATIONAL PARK CENTRES

Castleton
Cross Street (main car park).
Tel: 01433 620679

Edale
Fieldhead (right of road from
Edale Station to village).
Tel: 01433 670207

Fairholmes (Derwent Valley)
Tel: 01433 650953

PLACES OF INTEREST

Blue John Cavern
1m (1.6km) west of Castleton via
Winnats Pass
Tel: 01433 620638;
www.bluejohn-cavern.co.uk

Glossop Heritage Centre
Henry Street, Glossop.
Tel: 01457 869176

Last of the Summer Wine Exhibition
Huddersfield Road, Holmfirth.
Tel: 01484 681408

Peak Cavern
Castleton, village centre.
Tel: 01433 620285;
www.peakcavern.co.uk

Peveril Castle
Castleton.
Tel: 01433 620613

Saddleworth Museum
High Street, Uppermill.
Tel: 01457 874093;
www.saddleworthmuseum.co.uk

Speedwell Cavern
0.5 miles (0.8km) west of Castleton
at Winnats Pass.
Tel: 01433 620512;
www.speedwellcavern.co.uk

Treak Cliff Cavern
0.75 miles (1.2km) west of Castleton.
Tel: 01433 620571;
www.bluejohnstone.com

SHOPPING
Castleton
Farmers Market, first Sun each month.
Glossop
Indoor market, Thu.
Indoor and outdoor market, Fri and
Sat.
Holmfirth
Craft market, Sat and Bank Hols.
Farmers Market; 3rd Sun each month.
General market, Thu.

LOCAL SPECIALITIES
Blue John Jewellery
Speedwell Caverns Ltd,
Winnats Pass, Castleton.
Tel: 01433 620512
Also available from other local outlets.
Craft workshops
Glossop Craft Centre, No 1 Smithy
Fold, off High Street East, Glossop.
Tel: 01457 863559

SPORTS & ACTIVITIES
ANGLING
Arnfield Reservoir
Tintwistle. Tel: 01457 856269
BOAT TRIPS
Saddleworth
Pennine Moonraker Canal Cruises
Tel: 0161 652 6331;
www.saddleworth-canal-cruises.co.uk
CAVING
Edale
YHA Activity Centre, Rowland Cote,
Nether Booth.
Tel: 0870 770 5808;
www.yha.org.uk
Hathersage
Rock Lea Activity Centre, Station Road.
Tel: 01433 650345;
www.iain.co.uk
COUNTRY PARK
Etherow Country Park
George Street, Compstall, Stockport.
Tel: 0161 4276937
CYCLING
Longdendale Trail
A 6 mile (9.7km) multi-user trail
between Hadfield and the Woodhead
Tunnels.

DARK PEAK

The Sett Valley Trail
This trail runs for 2.5 miles (4km)
from New Mills to Hayfield.
CYCLE HIRE
Hayfield
Old Railway Station.
Tel: 01663 746222;
www.peakdistrict.org
GUIDED WALKS
Glossop
The walks (charge) last approximately
1.5 hours. They start from Glossop
Tourist Information Centre.
For details contact Glossop Tourist
Information Centre.
Tel: 01457 855920
National Park Walks with a Ranger
For more details contact the Peak
District National Park.
Tel: 01629 816200;
www.peakdistrict.org.uk
Peak District
Annual Peak District Walking Festival.
Large programme of guided walks held
in late Apr/early May.
Tel: 0870 444 7275;
www.visitpeakdistrict.com/walk

HORSE-RIDING
Edale
Lady Booth Riding Centre.
Tel: 01433 670205
LONG-DISTANCE
FOOTPATHS & TRAILS
The Limestone Way
A 46-mile (74km) route south from
Castleton through the White Peak to
Rocester (Staffordshire).
The Pennine Bridleway
Aimed at horse-riders and cyclists,
but also useful to walkers. A lengthy
350 miles (560km) from Cromford
via the Dark Peak to Byrness in
Northumberland.
The Pennine Way.
Runs for 256 miles (412km) from
Edale to Kirk Yetholm, just over the
border in Scotland.
The Sett Valley Trail
This trail runs for 2.5 miles (4km),
from New Mills to Hayfield.
The Trespass Trail
A 14-mile (22.6km) walk following the
route taken by the original trespassers
Hayfield on to Kinder Scout.

ROCK-CLIMBING

Edale

Edale YHA Activity Centre, Rowland
Cote, Nether Booth.
Tel: 0870 770 5808

Hathersage

Rock Lea Activity Centre, Peak
Activities Ltd, Station Road.
Tel: 01433 650345
www.iain.co.uk

WATERSPORTS

Hathersage

Rock Lea Activity Centre, Peak
Activities Ltd, Station Road.
Also helicopter rides.
Tel: 01433 650345;
www.iain.co.uk

ANNUAL EVENTS & CUSTOMS

For the full programme visit
www.visitpeakdistrict.com

Alport Castle

Alport Love Feast in Alport Barn.
Access via Heyridge Farm on A57,
early Jul.

Castleton

Garland Ceremony, 29 May.

Glossop

Jazz Festival, mid-Jun. Carnival
and Country Fair, early Jul.
Victorian weekend, early Sep.
Well dressing and Padfield Plum Fair,
Sep.

Hayfield

Well dressing, mid July.
Sheepdog Trials, Sep

Holmfirth

Folk Festival, early May.

Hope

Well dressing, late Jun–early Jul.
Sheepdog Trials and Agricultural Show,
late Aug.

Saddleworth

Brass band contest, Whit Friday.
Folk Festival, late Jul.
Longwood Thump Rushcart Festival,
late Aug.

TEA ROOMS

Rose Cottage Café
Cross Street, Castleton,
Derbyshire, S33 8WH
Tel: 01433 620472
Climbing plants decorate the outside
of this traditional English teashop. At
the rear is a secluded patio. There's
an excellent choice of freshly prepared
food, including cream teas, grand
sandwiches, home-baked cakes,
steaming bowls of soup and coffee.

Grumbley's
Church Street, Hayfield,
Derbyshire, SK22 2JE
Tel: 01663 741444
www.grumbleys.com
This modern café-bar and bistro at
the heart of the village is popular with
walkers to Kinder. Renowned for its
inventive, modern cooking, there's also
a good range of snacks, pastries, cakes
and more substantial meals; in the
evenings it is a popular restaurant.

The Wrinkled Stocking Tea Room
Huddersfield Road, Holmfirth,
West Yorkshire, HD9 2JS
Tel: 01484 681408
www.wrinkledstocking.co.uk
Cool pastel walls and crisp tablecloths
– just what Nora Batty would expect!
Located at those famous steps at
Compo's house (now an exhibition),
indulge in home-baked speciality
pastries and cakes (try the parkin)
and good Yorkshire tea. Sid's Café
(Tel: 01484 689610) is a short stroll
away, near the church.

Woodbine Café
Castleton Road, Hope,
Derbyshire, S33 6AA
Tel: 01433 621407
A welcoming, homely stone terraced
cottage, with a sheltered tea garden,
not far from Hope's distinctive
church. Within it is cosy and tranquil,
appetizing aromas of home-baking
mingling with quiet conversation or the
crackle of logs on a winter fire. They
also offer B&B.

DRYSTONE WALL

The Church Inn
Pob Green, Uppermill,
Saddleworth, OL3 6LW
Tel: 01457 872415
Splendid food (try the savoury suet puddings) is twinned with tasty beers brewed in the cellar. Memorabilia from the Rushcart Festival held each August is scattered about. Views from this most welcoming gritstone pub, high above the Tame Valley are stunning. As you might guess from its name, it is situated next to the church.

Cheshire Cheese Inn
Edale Road, Hope,
Derbyshire, S33 6ZF
Tel: 01433 620381
www.cheshire-cheese.net
A compact, cheerful local with a warm welcome guaranteed. The landlord is keen on stocking beers from some of the Peak District's many microbreweries and offers an ever-changing menu using local produce whenever possible.

Pack Horse Inn
Mellor Road, New Mills,
Derbyshire, SK22 4QQ
Tel: 01663 742365
www.packhorseinn.co.uk
High above New Mills, the inn has an enviable position with views to the great moorland plateau of Kinder. It's a lovely stone-built place with a growing reputation for good wholesome food and an eclectic choice of real ales.

The Royal Hotel
Market Street, Hayfield,
Derbyshire, SK22 2EP
Tel: 01663 741721
At the hub of the village, this grandiose inn has a patio where you can enjoy the local beers and take in the views of Kinder Scout. Inside, find a peaceful corner and tuck in to filling pub grub – there's usually a good fish menu.

LAKE DISTRICT NATIONAL PARK INFORMATION POINT
Peak District National Park Headquarters
Head Office, Aldern House, Baslow Road, Bakewell. Tel: 01629 816200; www.peakdistrict.org.uk

OTHER INFORMATION
Angling
Numerous opportunities for fishing on farms, lakes and rivers. Permits and licences are available from local tackle shops and TICs.

Cheshire Wildlife Trust
Grebe House, Reaseheath, Nantwich, Cheshire. Tel: 01270 610180; www.wildlifetrust.org.uk

Derbyshire Wildlife Trust
East Mill, Bridge Foot, Belper, DE56 1HX. Tel: 01773 881188; www.derbyshirewildlifetrust.org.uk

English Heritage
Canada House, 3 Chepstow Street, Manchester. Tel: 0161 242 1400 www.english-heritage.org.uk

English Nature
"Endcliffe", Deepdale Business Park, Ashford Road, Bakewell, DE45 1GT. Tel: 01629 816640

Environment Agency
Manley House, Kestrel Way, Exeter. Tel: 08708 506 506

Longshaw Visitor Centre
Tel: 01433 631708

The National Trust
East Midlands Regional Office, Clumber Park Stableyard, Worksop, Nottinghamshire.
Tel: 01909 486377; www.nationaltrust.org.uk

Parking
Most urban and many rural car parks in Derbyshire and the Peak District area are pay and display. Period visitors' parking tickets are available to personal callers from National Park Visitor Centres and cycle hire centres, or you can apply in writing to the Peak District National Park Head Office at Bakewell, Derbyshire.

Places of Interest

We give details of just some of the facilities within the area covered by this guide. Further information can be obtained from local TICs or the web.

Public Transport

'Derbyshire Wayfarer' allows one day's unlimited travel on all local buses and trains. Details from Derbyshire County Council, Public Transport Dept.
Tel: 01629 580000
Bus services in Derbyshire
0870 608 2608; www.derbysbus.net
GMPTE Tel: 0161 228 7811;
SYPTE Tel: 01709 515151
Rail Information.
Tel: 08457 484950

Severn Trent Water

2297 Coventry Road, Birmingham.
Tel: 0121 7224968;
www.stwater.co.uk

Staffordshire Wildlife Trust

The Wolseley Centre, Wolseley Bridge, Stafford ST17 0WT.
Tel: 01889 880100;
www.staffordshirewildlife.org.uk

United Utilities Plc.

Dawson House, Great Sankey, Warrington, Cheshire.
Tel: 01925 234000;
www.unitedutilities.com

Weather

Tel: 0906 850 0412;
www.weathercall.co.uk

INDEX